*Merry Christmas Mom. Happy
Love, John*

CROSS COUNTRY
ski tours
IN CENTRAL OREGON

by
VIRGINIA MEISSNER

ISBN 0-9613755-1-5

Published by Meissner Books
P. O. Box 5296, Bend, OR 97708

Photos and maps are by the author

Cover photo - Mt. Bachelor as seen
   from Crater Ditch flat

Cross Country Ski Tours in Central Oregon
         © 1984
         All rights reserved

Lunch along the ski trail.

ACKNOWLEDGEMENTS

I would like to thank my family and friends who have helped to make this book possible with help and encouragement. Maxine Heise did the typing. Marshall LaCour was photo consultant and printed the black and white photographs. Forest Service employees from the Deschutes and Ochoco National Forests were trail consultants.

Also, thanks to all of the family, friends and students who have skied many, many miles of cross country ski trails with me.

INTRODUCTION

In this book, I have tried to introduce you to a wide variety of places to ski cross country. There are trails from very flat to difficult so all the family can find something to enjoy. I hope you will find some new trails which will become favorites. As you ski the various trails I hope you have as much fun as I have had over the years.

Trail descriptions have purposely been kept short and simple. The map included with each trail is a sketch map of the immediate area. It is recommended that USGS or USDA Forest Service maps will also be used. When snow covers the ground, trails are not always as easy to follow as a hiking trail in the summer. Some trails are well marked with blue diamonds on the trees and others are roads. Know where you are at all times.

When skiing through the woods without a marked trail, keep watch of where you are and look at the way back. The ski tracks you are making could be covered with new snow or crisscrossed with other tracks making it impossible to follow your trail back.

Maps of the Deschutes National Forest, Ochoco National Forest and Willamette National Forest are available at any of the Forest Service offices or Ranger Stations. Maps you might want are:
      Deschutes National Forest
      Willamette National Forest
      Ochoco National Forest
      Three Sisters Wilderness
      Mt. Washington Wilderness
      Mt. Jefferson Wilderness
      Diamond Peak Wilderness

Trail maps of immediate ski areas are often available at the district ranger stations in Bend, Sisters, Crescent, Oakridge and Prineville. Some sno-parks have printed trail maps on bulletin boards with posted maps at the trailheads.

If you have never skied before, sign up for a class and get started right. Proper instruction is important for enjoyment and safety.

Some important things to remember: tell someone at home where you are going and when you expect to return. DO NOT go alone. Check road, weather and snow conditions. Weather conditions can change rapidly and are one of the greatest dangers in winter. Dress for the weather with layers of clothing which can be put on and off.

A day pack is essential for basic survival items such as lunch, extra clothing and food, water, first aid equipment, map and compass, matches and fire starter, jack knife, sun glasses, sunscreen lotion, whistle, space blanket, plastic, wax, emergency ski tip and repair kit.

Try to leave the land the way you found it, or if possible, in better condition. Carry out all trash. Avoid activities which would pollute water in lakes and streams.

Resist the urge to drink from lakes or streams. They may no longer be pure because of giardia.

When snow comes, be ready, get out there, ski at your own speed, enjoy it and HAVE FUN!

Fog over Paulina Lake

CONTENTS

SECTION 1
CENTURY DRIVE
(Cascade Lakes Highway)

No.		Page
1.	Dutchman Flat	16
2.	Dutchman Flat Loop.	18
3.	Water Tower Trail to Todd Lake. . . .	20
4.	Choices at Todd Lake.	20
5.	Meadow Trail to Todd Lake	22
6.	Big Meadow Trail	24
7.	Upper Todd Trail	24
8.	Crater Ditch	26
9.	Flag Line (Dutchman Flat to Swampy Lakes)	28
10.	Southside Cinder Pit	30
11.	Sparks Lake	31
12.	Elk Lake	32
13.	Hosmer Lake	32
14.	Tumalo Mt.	34
15.	Vista	36
16.	Vista Lower Loop.	38
17.	Vista Butte Trail	38
18.	Vista Trail to Swampy Lakes	40
19.	Vista, South Side	41
20.	Swampy Lakes Sno-park	42
21.	Swampy Lakes - Main Trail	44
22.	Swampy Lakes Loop	46
23.	Beginner Loop	48
24.	Alternate Beginner Loop	49
25.	Ridge Loop	50
26.	Nordeen Shelter Loop.	52
27.	Swede Ridge Shelter	54
28.	Ridge and Vista Loop.	56
29.	Tangent Trailhead	58
30.	Tangent Choices	60
31.	Tangent Practice Hill	62
32.	Big Spring	64
33.	Kiwa Springs and Kiwa Butte	66
34.	Kiwa Springs via Road #41	67

SECTION 2
SOUTH FROM BEND

No.		Page
35.	Lava Butte	70
36.	Benham Falls	71
37.	Lava Cast Forest	72

SUNRIVER TO MT. BACHELOR

38.	Ann's Butte	76
39.	Road #4180	78
40.	Junction of Roads #40 and #45	80
41.	Junction of Roads #45 and #4025	82
42.	Edison Ice Cave	84
43.	Dutchman Creek	85

SOUTH CENTURY DRIVE

44.	South Twin Lake	86
45.	Loop Around North and South Twin Lakes	88
	Sheep Bridge Campground	88
46.	Cultus Lake	90
47.	Elk Lake from South Century Drive	92

SECTION 3
SKYLINER ROAD & TUMALO FALLS

48.	Cinder Pit - Skyliner Road	96
49.	Skyliner - Snowplay Area	98
50.	Tumalo Falls	100
51.	South Fork Shelter	103
52.	Cougar Ridge	104
53.	Jackpine Spring	104

SECTION 4
IN OR NEAR BEND

No.		Page
54.	Shevlin Park	108
55.	Skyline Park	110
56.	Drake Park	111
57.	Juniper Park	111

SECTION 5
NEWBERRY CRATER

58.	Paulina Lake Trail	114
59.	Paulina Peak	116
60.	Little Crater Campground	118
61.	East Lake	119

SECTION 6
THREE CREEK LAKE

62.	Three Creek Lake	122
63.	Little Three Creek Lake	124
64.	Tam McArthur Rim	126

SECTION 7
McKENZIE

65.	McKenzie - Lower Elevation Roads	130
66.	Dugout Lake	132
67.	McKenzie Pass	134
68.	Windy Point	136
69.	Dee Wright Observatory	136
70.	Lava Camp Lake	137

SECTION 8
SANTIAM PASS

No.		Page
71.	Suttle Lake	140
72.	Scout Lake Loops	142
73.	Corbett State Park	144
74.	Round Lake	146
75.	Corbett Sno-park	148
76.	Blue Lake Trail	149
77.	Ray Benson Sno-park	150
78.	North Loop Trail	152
79.	South Loop Trail	153
80.	Big Lake	154
81.	Little Nash	156
82.	Potato Hill	158
83.	Big Meadow	160
84.	Fay Lake	160

SECTION 9
WILLAMETTE PASS

85.	Rosary Lakes	164
86.	Pacific Crest Trail Loop	166
87.	Gold Lake	168
88.	Marilyn Lake	169
89.	Pengra Pass Trails	170
90.	Maklaks	172
91.	Fawn Lake from Crescent Lake	174
92.	Fawn Lake from Odell Lake	175
93.	Odell Meadows	176
94.	Odell Butte	177

SECTION 10
OCHOCOS

No.		Page
95.	Bandit Spring	180
96.	Southside - Marks Creek	181
97.	Crystal Springs	182
98.	Walton Lake	184
99.	Road 200 - Blue Ridge Mine, Round Butte	186
100.	Lookout Mountain	188
	Resorts and Ski Areas with Cross Country Ski Trails	191

Mt. Bachelor from Upper Todd Meadow

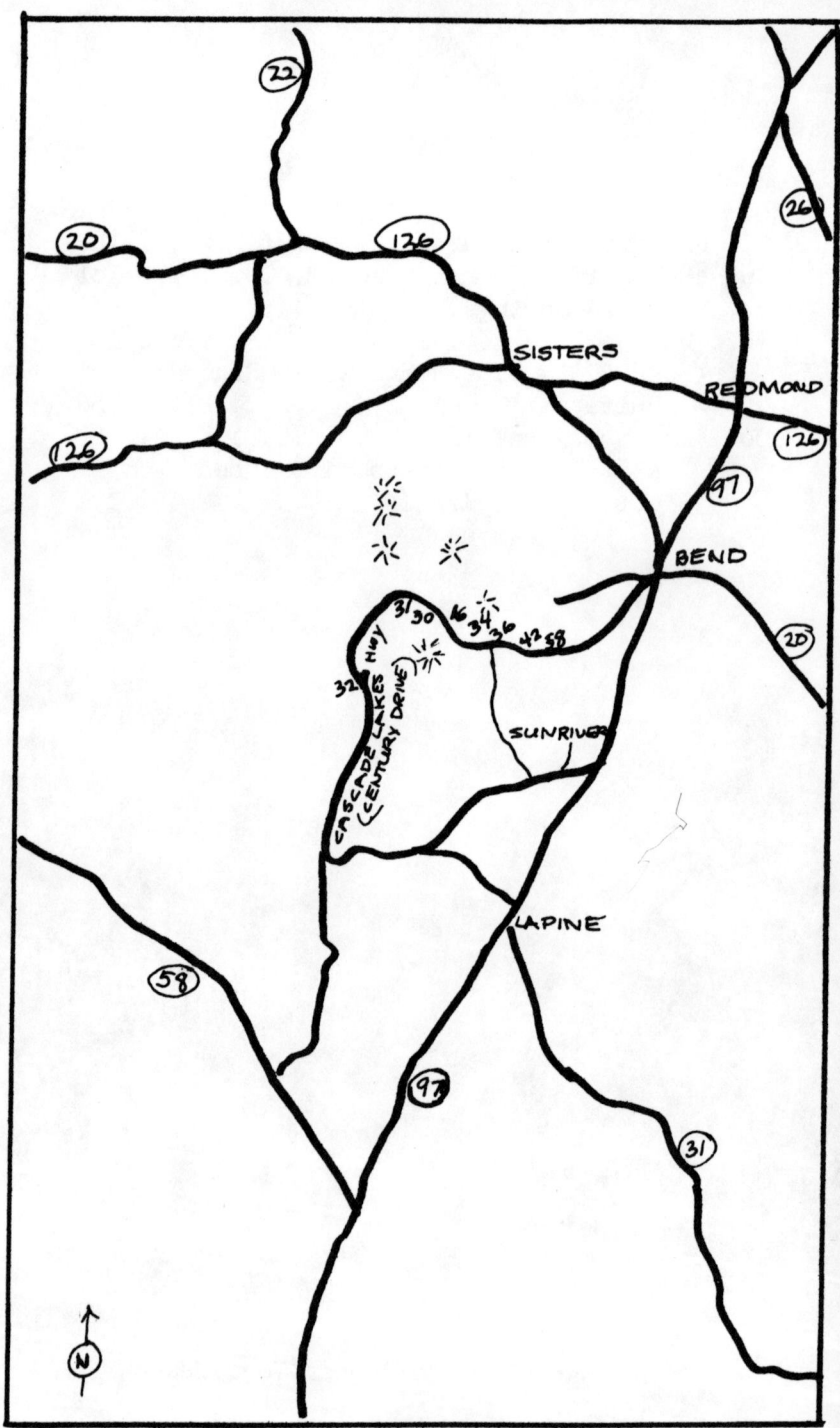

SECTION 1
CENTURY DRIVE
(Cascade Lakes Highway)

No.		Page
1.	Dutchman Flat	16
2.	Dutchman Flat Loop	18
3.	Water Tower Trail to Todd Lake	20
4.	Choices at Todd Lake	20
5.	Meadow Trail to Todd Lake	22
6.	Big Meadow Trail	24
7.	Upper Todd Trail	24
8.	Crater Ditch	26
9.	Flag Line (Dutchman Flat to Swampy Lakes)	28
10.	Southside Cinder Pit	30
11.	Sparks Lake	31
12.	Elk Lake	32
13.	Hosmer Lake	32
14.	Tumalo Mountain	34
15.	Vista	36
16.	Vista Lower Loop	38
17.	Vista Butte Trail	38
18.	Vista Trail to Swampy Lakes	40
19.	Vista, South Side	41

Three Fingered Jack as seen
from the Airstrip Burn.

CENTURY DRIVE

(Cascade Lakes Highway)

Cont.

20. Swampy Lakes Sno-park 42
21. Swampy Lakes - Main Trail 44
22. Swampy Lakes Loop 46
23. Beginner Loop 48
24. Alternate Beginner Loop 49
25. Ridge Loop. 50
26. Nordeen Shelter Loop 52
27. Swede Ridge Shelter 54
28. Ridge and Vista Loop 56
29. Tangent Trailhead 58
30. Tangent Choices 60
31. Tangent Practice Hill 62
32. Big Spring 64
33. Kiwa Springs and Kiwa Butte 66
34. Kiwa Springs via Road #41 67

1 DUTCHMAN FLAT

STARTING POINT: Drive west from Bend on the Cascade Lakes Highway (Century Drive) #46 for about 20 miles to the Dutchman Flat backcountry Sno-park. This is on the right of the highway, across from Mt. Bachelor.

DISTANCE: Choice of any distance you want on the various trails.

ELEVATION: About 6,300' at the parking lot
Todd Lake: about 6,150'
Big Meadow: about 6,560'
Crater Ditch: about 6,800'

TERRAIN: Very easy on Dutchman Flat to difficult on the ridges.

MAPS: USDA Forest Service: Three Sisters Wilderness map
USGS: Broken Top, Oregon, 15' 1959

The Dutchman Flat area is an area of much use by a variety of cross country skiers. There are many marked ski trails which go out from here. There are so many choices of trails and loop trips that I will not try to describe all of them. The following are some of the best. Maps are available from the forest service or at the trailhead box.

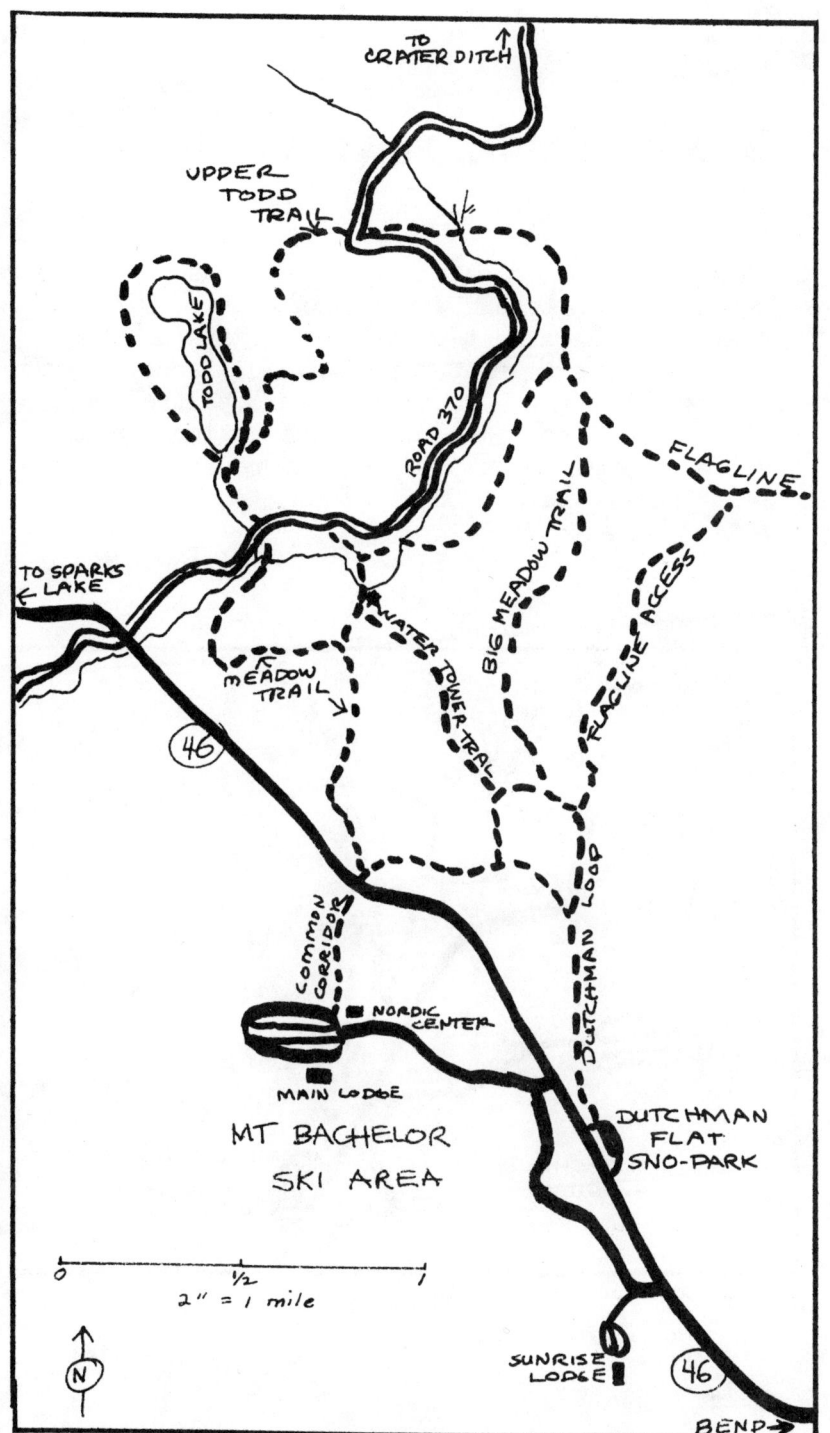

2 DUTCHMAN FLAT LOOP

This is a wide open flat. It extends for over a mile in length and varies in width. Dutchman Flat is an excellent place for beginning skiers because it is so flat for such a distance. There is usually a good ski trail around the outer edge which can be used to practice diagonal glide. By skiing around the outer edges, it is possible to make a flat loop of more than two miles.

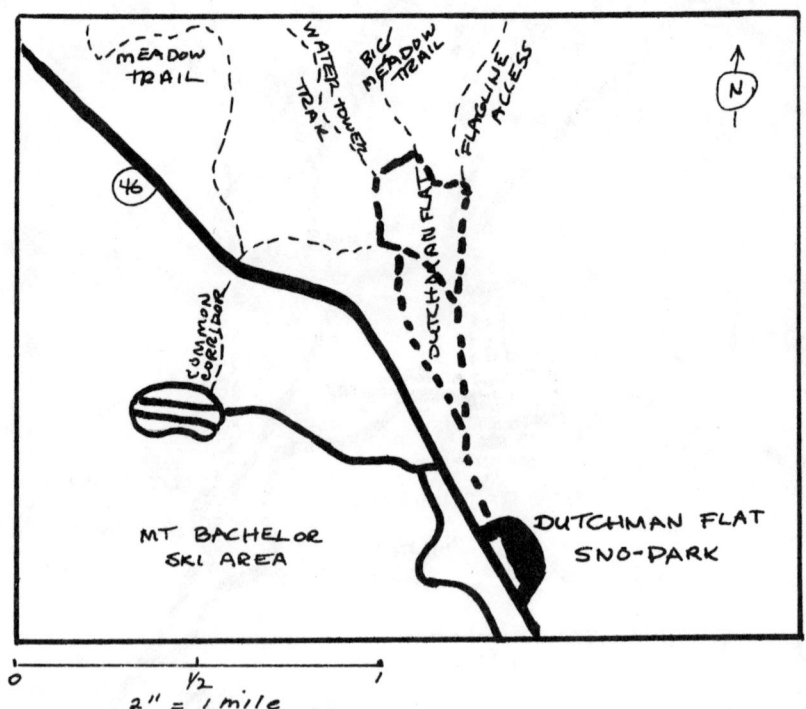

Mountain view from Dutchman Flat.

3 WATER TOWER
TRAIL TO TODD LAKE

Follow the Dutchman Flat loop to the right, almost a mile to the junction with the Flag Line Access trail which goes to the right. These trails are usually marked with blue bamboo poles. There are signs at the junctions. Go on across the flat to the trees.

The trail starts uphill into the trees. Soon there is a junction with the Big Meadow trail. Go left for a short distance and then right on the next trail, which is the Dutchman Trail to the water tower. (The "water tower" is the water intake for the Mt. Bachelor water system.) This is at upper Todd meadow.

At the water tower, cross the meadow (bridge is over by the water tower if snow does not already make a snow bridge across the creek) and ski uphill to road 370. Ski left down the road to Todd Lake junction and right up to the lake.

4 CHOICES AT TODD LAKE

1. Ski around the lake. Follow the edge of the lake just back from lake level. Be extra careful around the outlet and at the far end where small streams run into the lake.

2. Ski left across the bridge and follow a road uphill through the trees to the far end of the lake. At the upper end of Todd Lake are open slopes. Some are steep, others very gentle so that most everyone can find a hill to his liking.

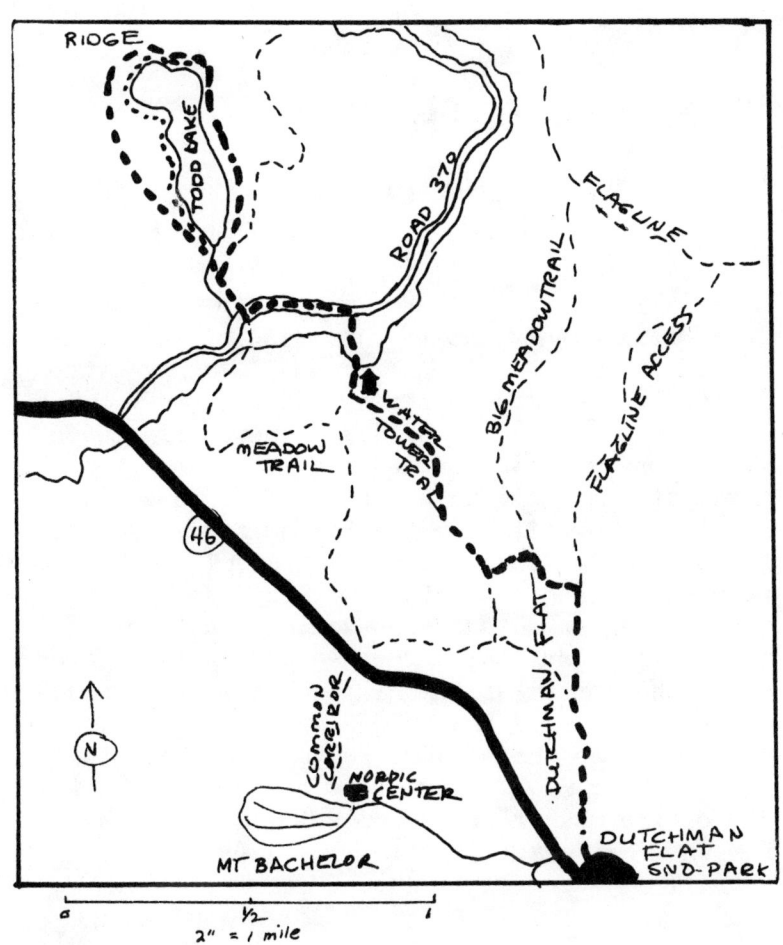

3. Climb the ridge. At the far end of Todd Lake is a steep ridge. Check out the snow conditions before you start up. At times icy conditions or heavy, deep snow make it unsafe. Good snow and a sunny day make this a nice climb. From the top of the ridge there is an excellent view across to the South Sister and Broken Top and all of the country in between.

5 MEADOW TRAIL

TO TODD LAKE

This trail starts at the junction of the Common Corridor from Mt. Bachelor and Century Drive. It can be reached by skiing down Century Drive (stay to the side as this is a snowmobile route) or around across Dutchman Flat. The Meadow Trail starts out down a road. This is a fairly narrow, long hill, maybe one-half mile or so. At the bottom, the road becomes level, following near the edge of a ridge. Stay on the main trail straight ahead when you come to the water tower hill junction. The Meadow Trail goes on along the bottom of the ridge and drops down another hill to the Lower Todd meadow. Trail is marked across the meadow to the Todd Lake junction on Road 370. There is a bridge in the middle of the meadow if the snow is not deep enough for snow bridges.

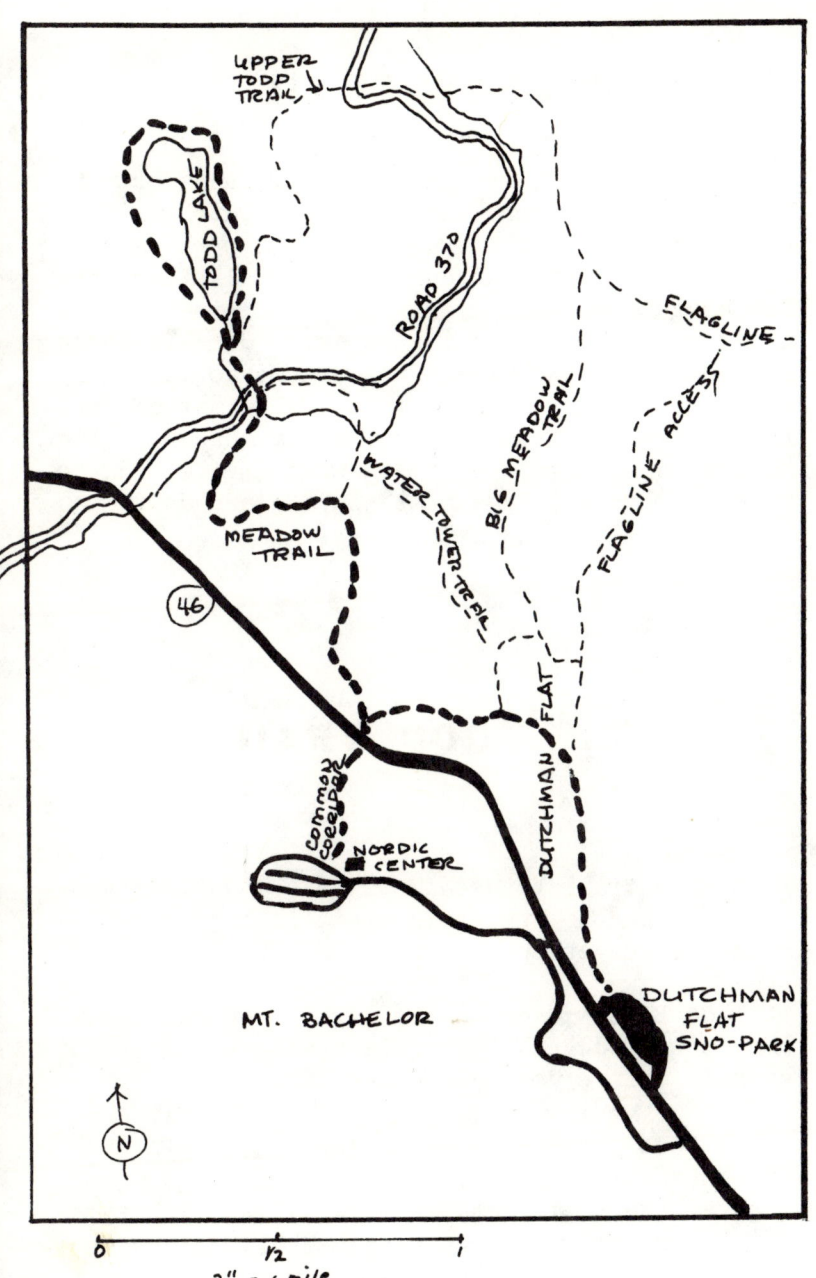

6 BIG MEADOW TRAIL

This trail can be reached from Mt. Bachelor via the Common Corridor, or from the Dutchman Flat Sno-park. From the Dutchman Flat parking area go right, down Dutchman Flat, following the Dutchman Loop Trail past the Flag Line access trail and uphill into the woods. Shortly there will be a junction where the Big Meadow is marked to the right. This is a well marked and fairly easy climb up to the Big Meadow. Big Meadow is a large open flat with a view back to Mt. Bachelor and Tumalo Mt. on a clear day.

7 UPPER TODD TRAIL

This is a trail between Todd Lake and Big Meadow. The best way to ski this trail is clockwise because of the steep hill near Todd Lake.

At Todd Lake, keep to the right of the creek. The Upper Todd marked trail starts to the right shortly before you get to the lake.

From Todd Lake, the trail climbs quite steeply up through the trees. As it winds among the trees, the trail gets more level near the top of the ridge. From there the trail opens out into the upper end of Big Meadow. To complete the loop, ski across Big Meadow and return on the Big Meadow Trail to Dutchman Flat.

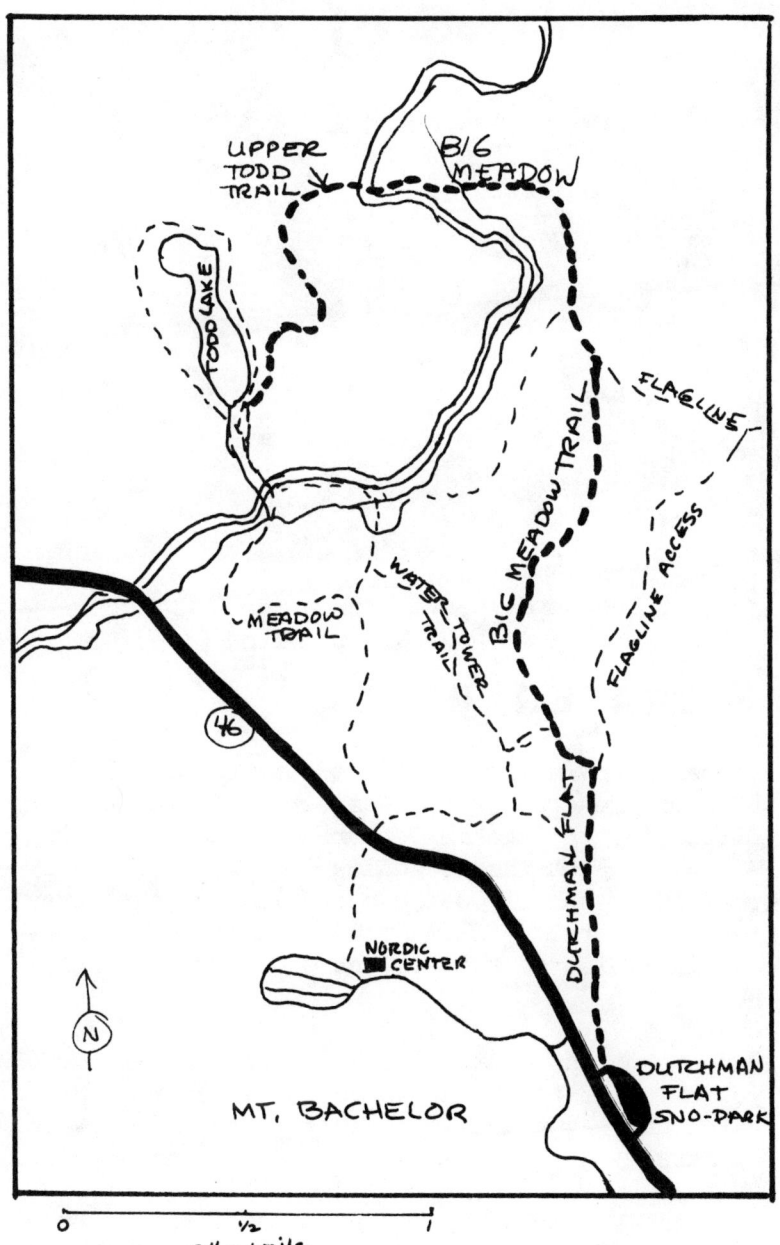

South Sister & Broken Top
from Crater Ditch Flat.

8 CRATER DITCH

There is no marked trail to any of the area above Big Meadow. The easiest way to Crater Ditch and the Broken Top area is to ski to Big Meadow. From there, follow road #370 (formerly road 1534) uphill to the open flats of the Crater Ditch area. This road is a groomed snowmobile trail so stay to one side and ski carefully.

Once up on the flat, there are nice views and you are free to ski anywhere. Use your map and watch where you are so that the return trip will be safe.

This is the access to wilderness skiing to Broken Top, Ball Butte, Green Lakes and McArthur Rim. Much of this high country in the wilderness is closed to motorized vehicles and is excellent for snow camping trips

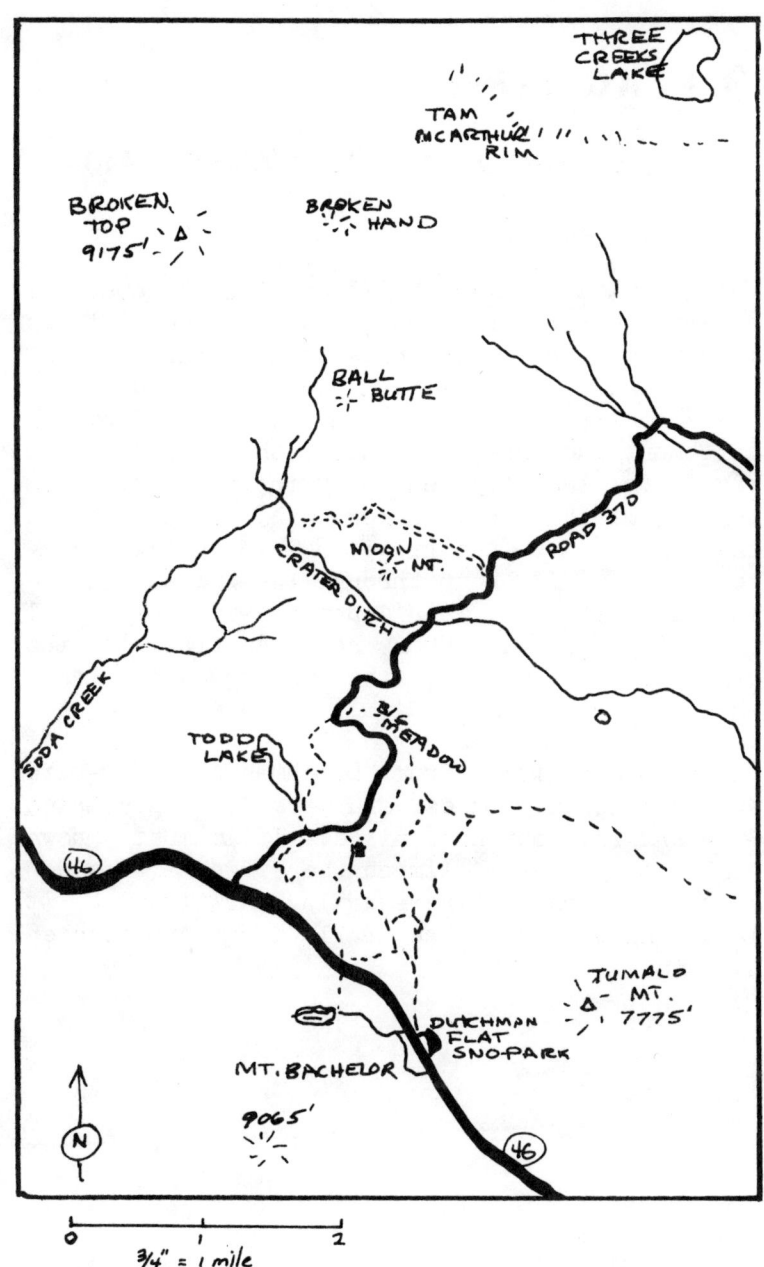

9 FLAG LINE

DUTCHMAN FLAT to SWAMPY LAKES

This trail is called the "Flag Line" because for several years when it was first in use, it was marked only with blue plastic ribbons tied on the trees. It has since been marked with ski trail markers, but the name remains. From the Dutchman Flat Sno-park follow the trail to the right to the far end of Dutchman Flat. From this point the trail marker will direct you to the right and up the ridge. The trail winds around as it climbs up through the trees. At the top of the ridge, is a junction with the trail from Big Meadow. From here the trail to the right is marked all the way to Swampy Lakes shelter.

The complete trail from Dutchman Flat Sno-park around to Swampy Lakes and back to Swampy Lakes Sno-park is about nine miles. It is mostly down hill once you have climbed the ridge. Consider snow conditions before starting this trail. It is a long way to break trail if there is deep new snow.

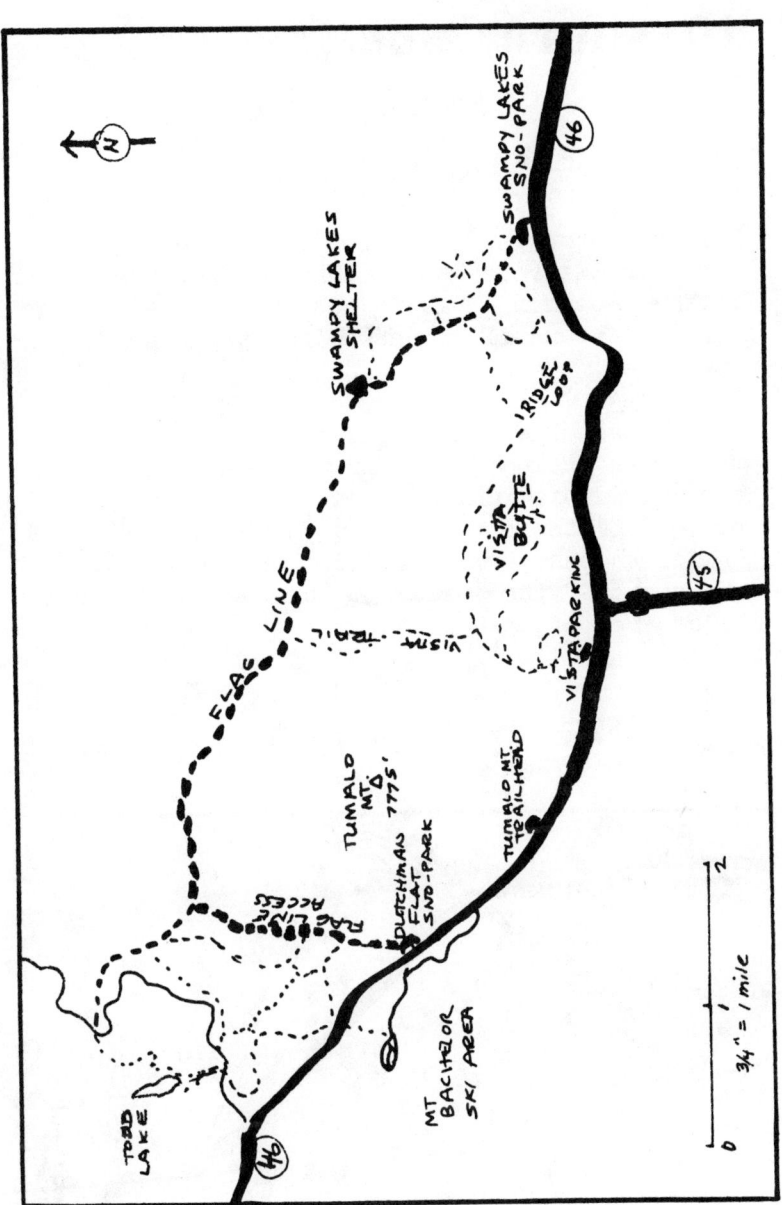

10 SOUTH SIDE
CINDER PIT

Follow Century Drive to Todd Lake Junction. Opposite the road to Todd Lake, there is a road to the south. This is not marked and is not easy to see until it enters the trees across the open flat.

Ski across the flat to where the stream enters the trees. The road is on the right of the stream. This road goes back into a big cinder pit. From there there is a butte to be climbed. Or for an easy trip, follow the road along on the right of the stream to the back of the butte to an area of open hills.

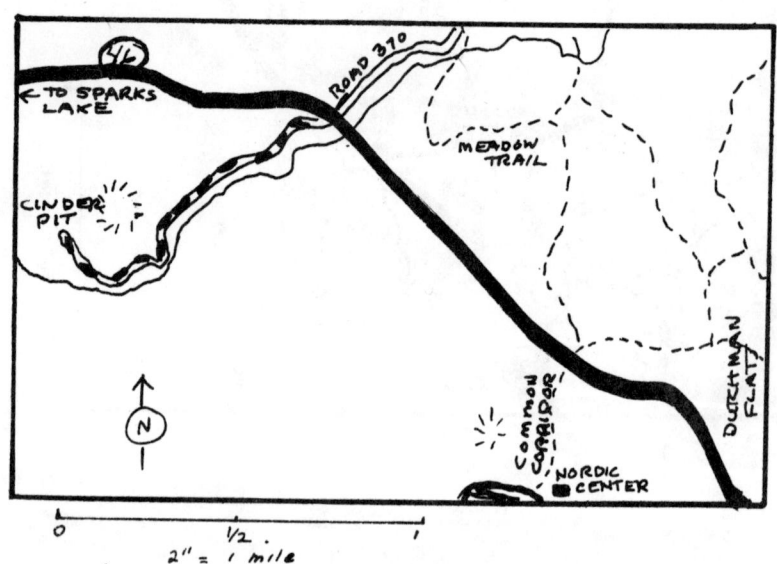

11 SPARKS LAKE

Starting either from Dutchman Flat Sno-park or from Mt. Bachelor Nordic Center, the trail to Sparks Lake is down the Century Drive. This road is shared with the snowmobiles and the snow cat from Elk Lake. Ski to one side, with all members of the party on the same side.

It is mainly downhill to Todd Lake junction. The road this far will also probably be groomed by the snowmobile packer.

From Todd Lake junction it is downhill for at least another two miles to Soda Creek where it becomes level into the meadow at Sparks Lake.

At Sparks Lake, there are very nice views of Mt. Bachelor, South Sister and Broken Top.

Remember that when you ski down to Sparks Lake it is mostly uphill coming back!

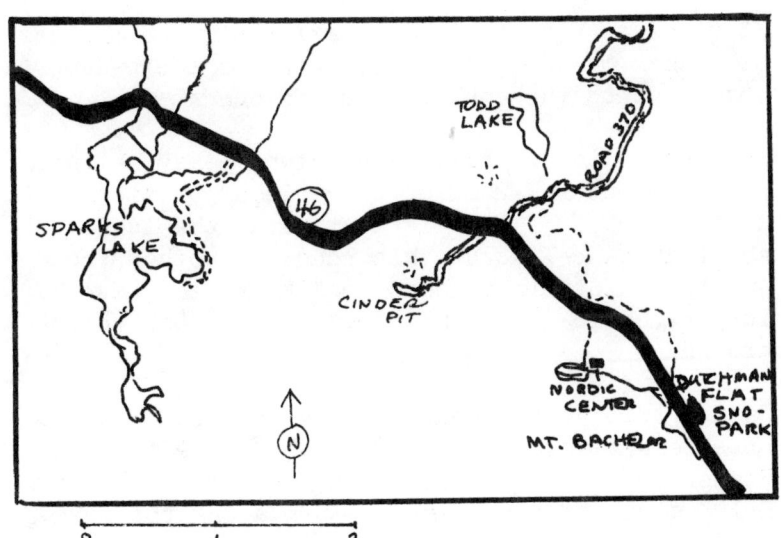

12 ELK LAKE

This is about an eleven mile trip from the Dutchman Flat Sno-park. Follow Century Drive to Sparks Lake. From there the road stays to the right of the meadow, crosses Fall Creek, and climbs slightly uphill into the lava. Then it drops downhill to Devils Lake. The road then turns to the south and on to Elk Lake. This last part is mainly downhill, but there are some level and short uphill sections.

Elk Lake Lodge remains open in the winter for snacks and meals. They also have cabins for rent in winter. It is well to reserve these in advance. The snow cat from Elk Lake also will take you in and out. It is a nice trip in one day to ski in and ride back out on the cat.

13 HOSMER LAKE

Starting at Elk Lake Lodge, ski clockwise around Elk Lake on the road which goes to the summer homes and to the east-side campgrounds.

The road is gentle up and down, easy skiing. After about 2 1/2 miles there is a junction for Hosmer Lake. Turn left toward the lake. A short distance down this road is another road junction. Straight ahead goes to Mallard Marsh. Turn right to go to the South Hosmer Lake campground.

Return trip can be back on the same road or as an alternative, continue on to the left at the Hosmer junction. This takes you out to Century Drive south of Elk Lake. Return along the road.

Total loop trip is about six miles.

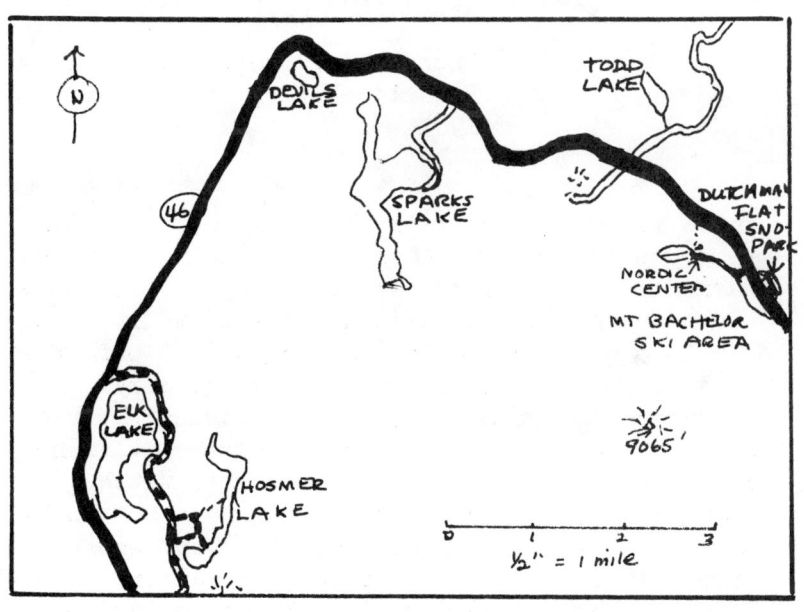

Skiers at Elk Lake

14 TUMALO MOUNTAIN

STARTING POINT: Drive west from Bend on the Cascade Lakes Highway (Century Drive) #46 for about 20 miles. Watch for a plowed turn-out on the right side (north). This is just shortly before the first Mt. Bachelor access road to the Sunrise Lodge.

DISTANCE: About 4 miles round trip

ELEVATION: Parking - about 6,200'
Top of Tumalo Mt. - 7,775'

TERRAIN: Steep (best done with good snow conditions)

MAPS: USDA Forest Service: Deschutes National Forest and Three Sisters Wilderness
USGS: Broken Top, Oregon, 15' 1959
Bachelor Butte, Oregon 7.5' 1963

There is no marked trail up Tumalo Mt. Be sure that you are able to keep your bearings in unmarked country before starting up here. On a clear, sunny day this is not so difficult, but should a storm close in before you get off the mountain, conditions could change quickly. Be prepared. Starting from the trailhead, the best way is to go straight up for a short way. Then start angling to the right. Then watch for openings in the trees and make traverses, working your way up the mountain. As you approach timberline, the slopes become much more open. Lots of really good downhill skiing coming back down.

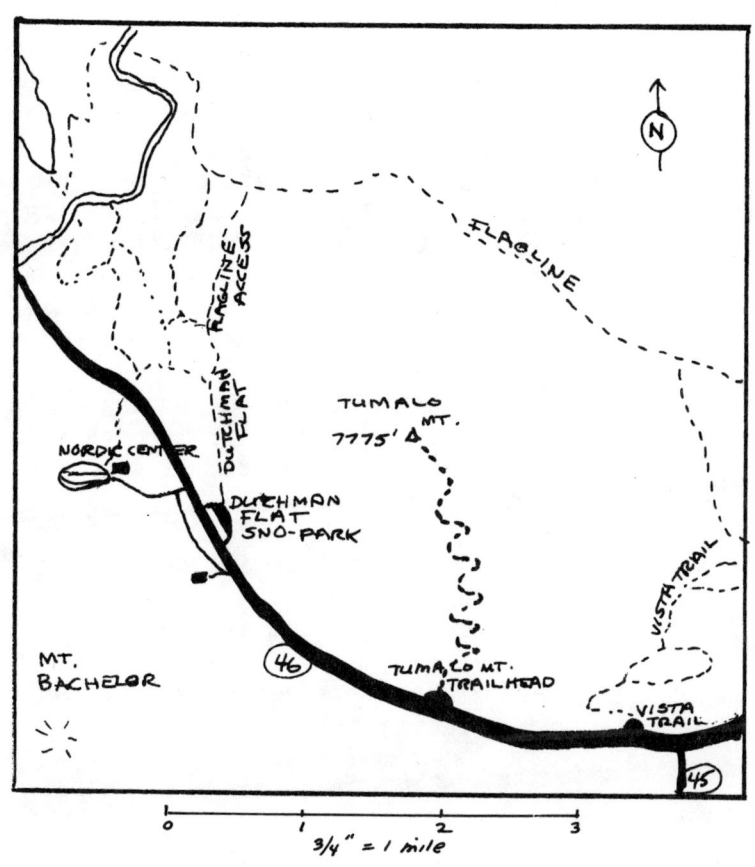

On top of Tumalo Mt. is an open ridge, offering excellent views in all directions. One word of caution on top, to the east and north-east there can be a rather large cornice which forms. This cannot be seen from above. Keep back away from the edge unless you are certain of what you are doing.

15 VISTA

STARTING POINT: Drive west from Bend on the Cascade Lakes Highway (Century Drive) #46. Several miles beyond the Swampy Lakes Nordic parking lot and just past the junction with the new Sun River road, there is a wide turn-out plowed for parking. This is Vista parking. (It is hoped that an enlarged parking area will be developed near here soon.) The trailhead sign is high on a tree above the parking. See note on page 39.

DISTANCE: Choice of distance depending upon which trails or loops. Some nice open spots are just above the first steep hill climb.

ELEVATION: About 5,900' at parking area

TERRAIN: Moderate to difficult

MAPS: USDA Forest Service: Deschutes National Forest map
USGS: Wanoga Butte, Oregon 7.5' 1963
Broken Top, Oregon 15' 1959

This is a new area of trails built mainly by volunteers from Bend. A marked ski trail starts on the north side of the highway. (Sometimes there is a high snowbank to climb up from the parking.)

The first part of this trail angles to the left through the trees and then begins to climb. Just before the trail comes to the snowmobile road, the trail takes a sharp curve back to the right. From here there is a traverse up a steep hillside. Once over the top of this, there is some very gentle terrain and nice open slopes.

Bruce's Ballpark

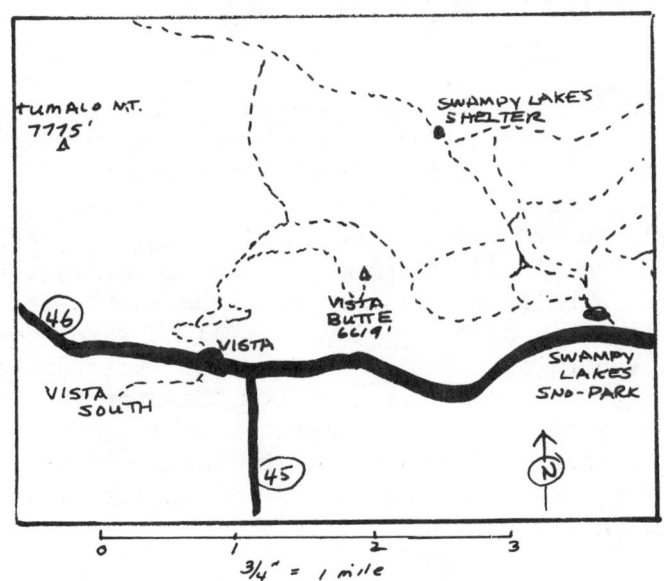

16 VISTA LOWER LOOP

Once up the first hillside traverse you enter an area of nice open slopes. Just over the ridge is a junction. This is the lower loop. Most of it is very gentle. The loop is best skied counter clockwise. At the junction sign, go right. From here the marked trail goes slightly down across the open. Then it follows a road for a while and eventually angles up through the trees to an upper level bench. It continues across this almost level area to a junction with the trail which goes on up the butte. Turn left to return back downhill and complete the loop.

17 VISTA BUTTE TRAIL

At the first junction just over the ridge hill climb, the main Vista Butte trail goes straight ahead. It is well marked up the ridge. The Vista lower loop trail comes in from the right on the second bench. Go straight ahead. From here the trail climbs up the main ridge to "Bruce's Ballpark". (This open area at the trail junction was named for Bruce Kirkland when these trails were being built.) To climb Vista Butte, 6,619', go to the right. From the top of the butte is one of the best views around. Not only do you see Mt. Bachelor, South Sister and Broken Top, but you can also look down on the Swampy Lakes and Tumalo Falls country.

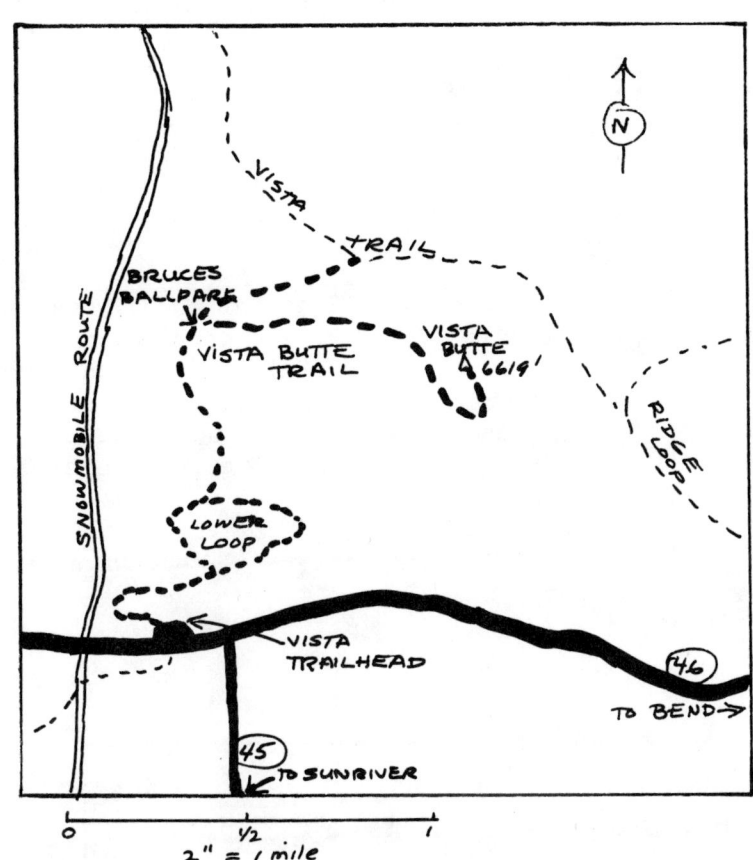

NOTE:
As this book goes to press a new <u>Vista Sno-park</u> is being built. It will be on the north side of the Cascade Lakes Highway (Century Drive) #46, just before the junction with Sunriver road #45.

Vista Sno-park will replace parking at the old double-wide roadside parking place. Park here for skiing tours # 15, 16, 17, 18. 19 and possibly for # 43.

18 VISTA TRAIL
to SWAMPY LAKES

Follow the Vista Butte trail as far as "Bruce's Ballpark". At this junction, go straight ahead and over the ridge. As the trail drops down the other side, it will soon join the Vista trail. At this point, there is a choice. To the left will take you to the Flag Line and then to Swampy Lakes Shelter. To the right will take you to the Swampy Lakes parking lot via the ridge loop. These trails back in here go through some very nice open woods.

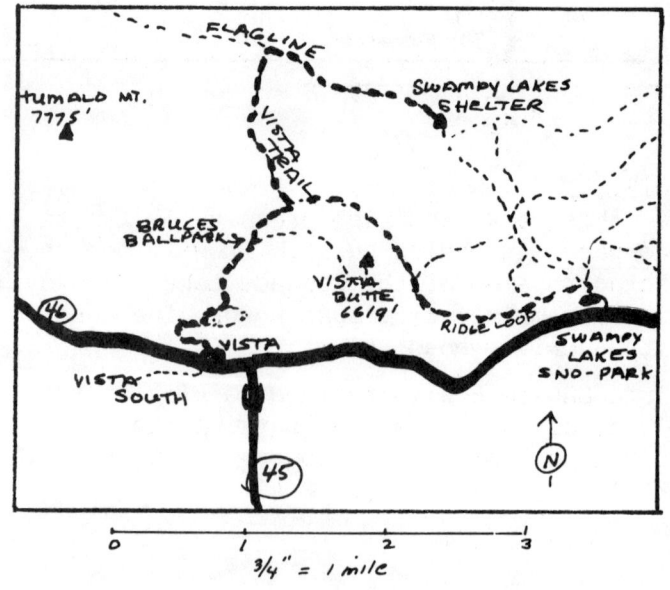

19 VISTA - SOUTH SIDE

Across the highway from the main Vista trailhead there is some nice, easy terrain for skiing. There are no marked trails here as yet. Just across from the parking and into the woods to the right is a road which is easy to follow. After about 1/2 mile, off to the south, there are some open slopes which are good practice hills. From here you can ski up Dutchman Creek (not marked) or down into the open flats. This is snowmobile country but there are always places to be found to ski.

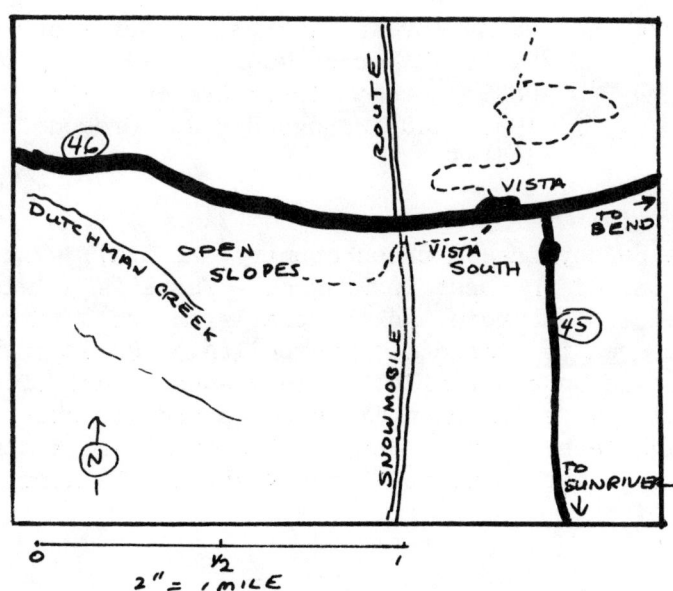

20 SWAMPY LAKES SNO-PARK

STARTING POINT: Drive west from Bend on the Cascade Lakes Highway (Century Drive) #46 for about 15 miles to the Swampy Lakes Nordic Sno-park area. It is on the north side of the highway. Marked ski trails begin at the end of the parking lot by the rest rooms. An open front shelter is near the trailhead.

DISTANCE: This area has a wide variety of trails and loops to choose from. Plan your distance according to ability, time of day and snow conditions.

ELEVATION: About 5,700' at the parking lot

TERRAIN: Easy to fairly difficult, depending upon snow conditions.

MAPS: USDA Forest Service: Deschutes National Forest Map
USGS: Broken Top, Oregon 15' 1959 and Wanoga Butte, Oregon 7.5' 1963

The Swampy Lakes cross country ski trail system is one of the best in Oregon. There is a wide choice of terrain and the trails are well marked. The area is closed to snowmobiles. No dogs are allowed on the trails. The weather here often will be good when it is too stormy to ski at higher elevations. Some trails from here interconnect with Dutchman Flat, Vista and Tangent.

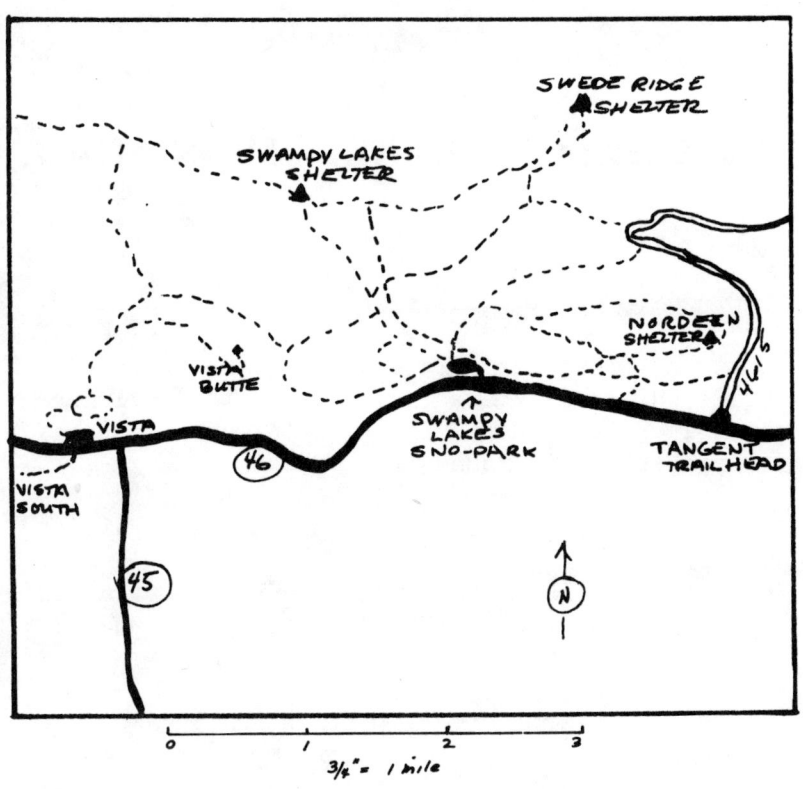

21 SWAMPY LAKES - MAIN TRAIL

DISTANCE: About 2 miles one way to the shelter.

Most of this trail is easy. There are a few hills which will be a challenge to the beginner. In most places there is room through the trees to traverse out around if desired.

This is the original, first marked, ski trail to Swampy Lakes. On a busy day it is well used. From the trailhead the trail starts out straight ahead, slightly downhill. At the first junction (soon) go to the left.

There are several other trails which turn off of the main trail, so check with your map if you are uncertain. Ski trail maps are usually available in the box at the trailhead.

When you reach the hill at Swampy Lake proceed with care, down the hill and follow the trail across the lake. The shelter is across the lake and about 1/4 mile back into the trees. Wood supply at the shelter is cut in the fall by volunteers and must last all winter, so use with moderation.

At lunch time there is uaually an abundance of birds begging for part of your lunch.

Skiers cross Swampy Lakes

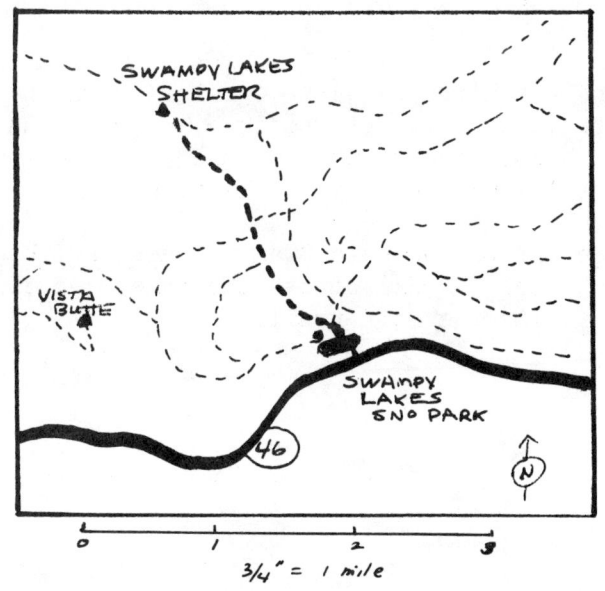

22 SWAMPY LAKES LOOP

DISTANCE: About 2 miles one way to the shelter. Loop is about 4 miles.

Most of this trail is easy. Some of it is quite narrow through the trees, but it is gentle rolling terrain.

This loop can be skied either way. I prefer going counter-clockwise. (It seems like there is more downhill going that way!)

From the trailhead go straight ahead, slightly downhill. At the first junction (soon) stay to the right going uphill to the four-way junction. Turn left at this four corners.

This is a road which climbs gently around a butte about 3/4 of a mile. The trail from there to the lake is rolling up and down through the woods.

Upon reaching the lake, go left down the lake. There is a view of Tumalo Mt. from the lake. The shelter is at the west end of the lake and about 1/4 mile back into the trees.

To return on the main Swampy Trail, ski back out to the lake. Ski across the lake, up the hill and follow the main trail.

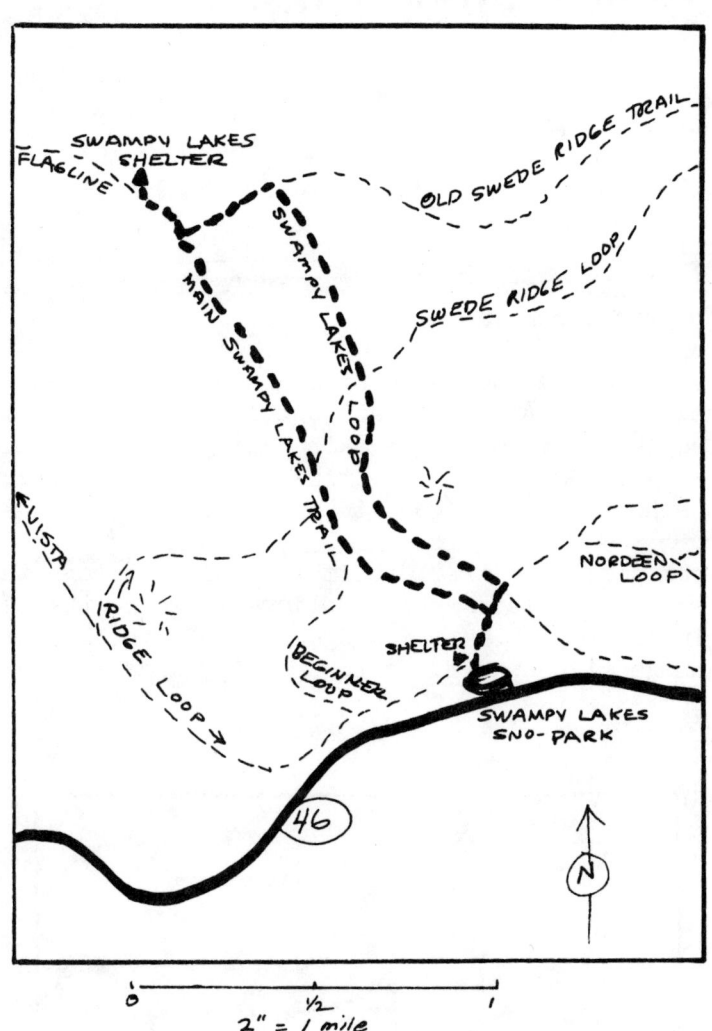

23 BEGINNER LOOP

DISTANCE: About 2 miles around the loop.

This is an easy trail. It is a pretty trail mostly through the trees. Preferred direction: counter-clockwise.

From the trailhead go straight ahead, slightly downhill. At the first junction (soon) go to the left. This is the main Swampy Trail. Follow this trail for 1/2 mile to a junction where the Beginner Loop goes to the left.

From here the trail climbs gently through the trees. A flat section follows to where the Beginner Loop joins the Ridge Loop. Go to the left and gently downhill to the parking area.

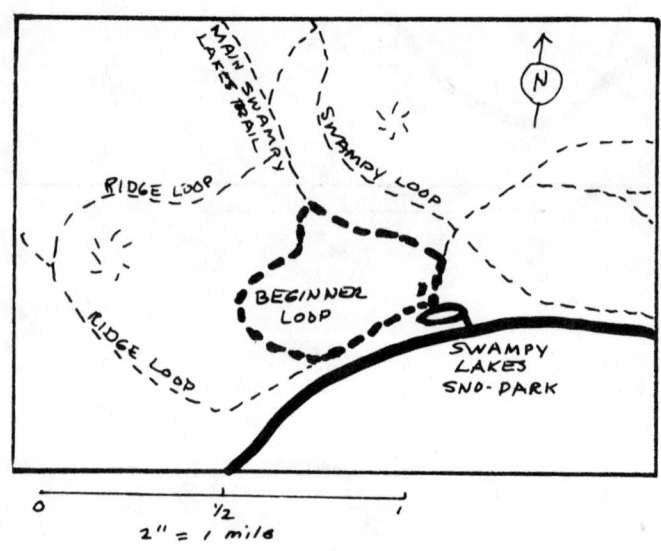

24 Alternate BEGINNER LOOP

DISTANCE: About 2 or 2 1/2 miles around the loop.

This is a very easy trail. Preferred direction: clockwise.

From the trailhead go straight ahead, slightly downhill.   At the first junction (soon) go to the left on the main Swampy Trail. Stay on this trail past the Beginner junction and past the Ridge Loop junction.

Shortly past the junction, where the Ridge Loop turns off, and part way down a small hill take the trail to the right.   About 1/2 mile up this trail is a four-way junction. Turn right.

From here follow the trail back to another four-way junction.   Turn right back to the parking lot.

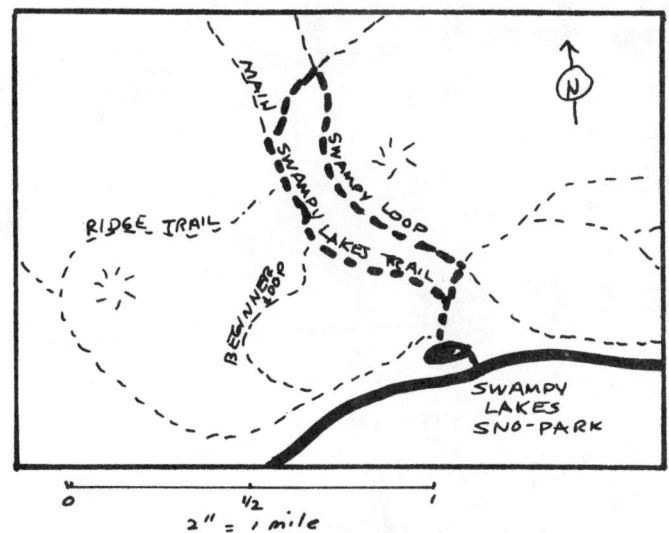

49

25 RIDGE LOOP

DISTANCE: About 3 miles around the loop.

Moderately easy unless snow conditions are icy. The trail climbs to a high point then is downhill coming back. Preferred direction: counter clockwise.

From the trailhead go straight ahead, slightly downhill. At the first junction (soon) go to the left on the main Swampy Trail. Follow this trail, past the junction where the Beginner Loop turns off, up a hill to the second junction. The Ridge Loop takes off to the left. From here the trail climbs up the ridge. There is a viewpoint part way up the ridge. Almost to the high part of the ridge, the Vista Loop Trail turns off to the right. Continue straight ahead.

Where the trail levels out near the top of the ridge is a fairly open slope which is good for telemark practice.

The trail from here back to the parking lot is mainly downhill.

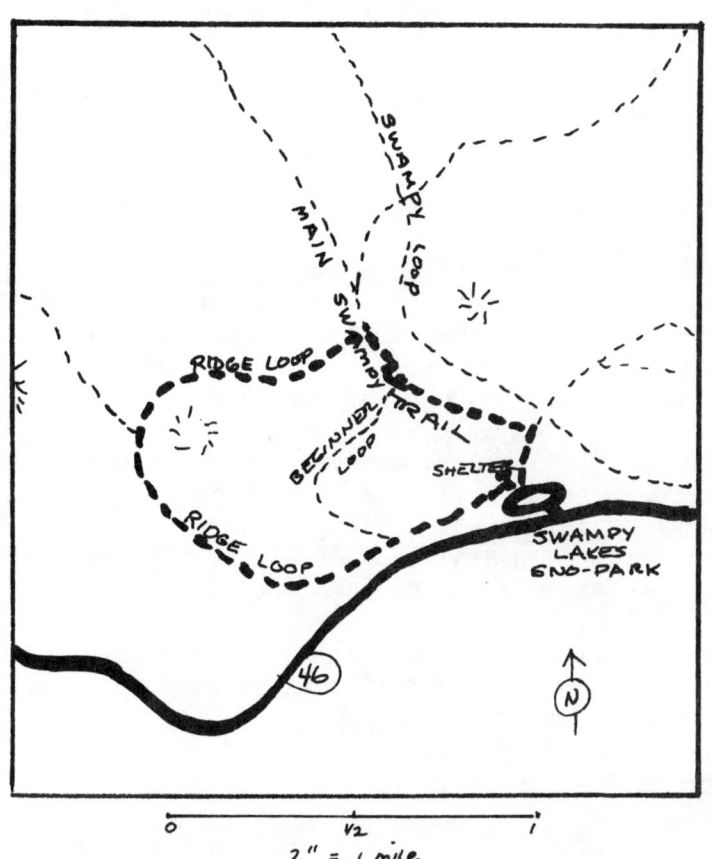

26 NORDEEN SHELTER LOOP

DISTANCE: About 5 1/2 miles around the loop.

This is a moderately easy trail: some through the woods, some open slopes. Preferred direction: clockwise.

From the trailhead go straight ahead, slightly downhill. At the first junction (soon) go to the right up the hill. Continue straight on up the hill at the four way junction.

As the trail breaks over the top of the hill the Nordeen Loop Trail goes to the right. About 1/2 mile on this trail is a junction. Both trails go to Nordeen Shelter. Go either way. I prefer going left and making the loop clockwise.

This shelter was built in 1980 and dedicated to Bend's veteran cross country ski racer, Emil Nordeen. There is an excellent view of the Lava Butte area and Newberry Crater from this shelter on top of a ridge.

On the trail west of the shelter are some open slopes which are great for telemark skiing. Continue on around the loop to the loop junction and back to the parking lot on the same trail you started out on.

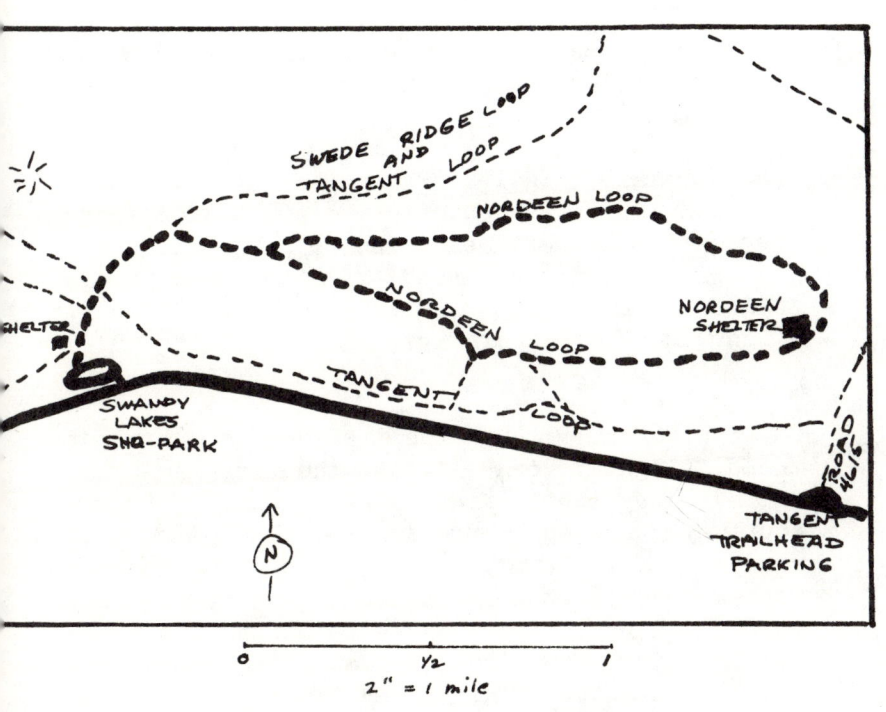

27 SWEDE RIDGE

DISTANCE: Depends upon which trail or loop trip you take. Plan on about seven miles round trip.

There are three trails which lead to Swede Ridge shelter. All are marked trails:

OLD SWEDE RIDGE TRAIL: Reach this trail by skiing to Swampy Lakes on either trail. From there proceed to the north-east end of the lake where you will find the marked trail to Swede Ridge shelter. Parts of this trail can be difficult if snow conditions are icy.

SWEDE RIDGE LOOP: From the trailhead go straight ahead, slightly downhill. At the first junction (soon) stay to the right, going uphill to the four-way junction. Turn left here. Follow this road and trail about 3/4 of a mile to another four-way junction. The trail to the right leads to Swede Ridge. About 1/2 mile before the shelter is a junction with the road which comes from the Tangent Loop. This is my favorite way to go.

TANGENT LOOP APPROACH: This route can be started either from the Swampy Lakes parking lot or from Tangent. From the Swampy Lakes parking lot go straight ahead. At the first junction (soon) stay right going uphill. At the four-way junction, keep going straight ahead and on up the hill. From the top of this ridge is a long downhill of more than a mile. At the bottom of the hill go left on the road. There is another junction after about 1/4 mile. Turn left again. The last junction before the shelter is a right turn on to the road into the shelter.

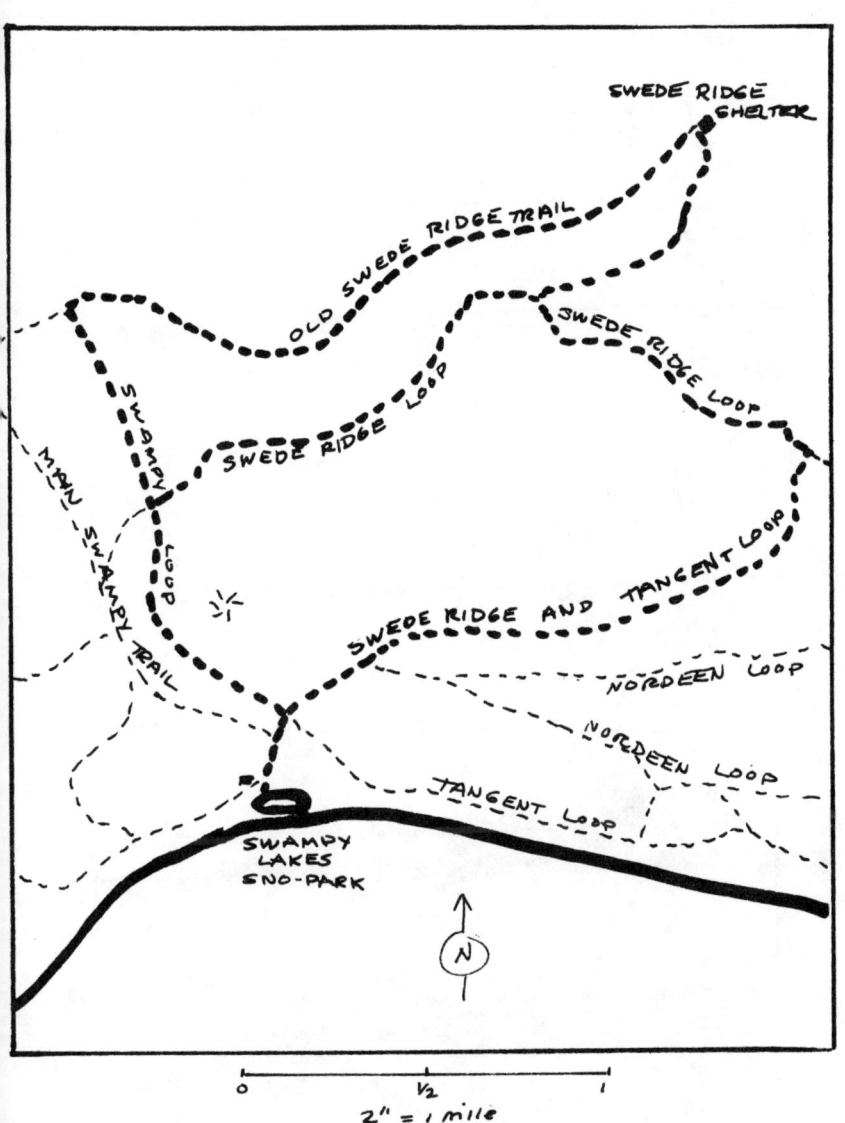

28 RIDGE & VISTA LOOP

DISTANCE: about seven miles around the loop.

Follow the directions for the Ridge Loop trail almost to the high part of the trail to the junction of the Vista Loop trail. The Vista trail from here is quite gentle, going through some nice open woods. Where the Vista Butte trail joins, stay to the right. Another mile and a quarter through open woods takes you to the Flag Line from Dutchman Flat. Turn right here. The trail is mainly downhill back to Swampy Lakes Shelter. From the shelter take either trail back out to the parking lot.

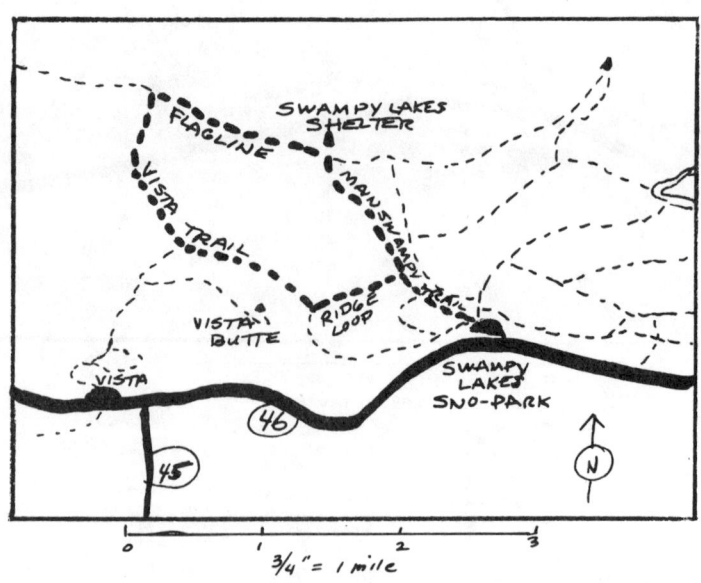

Broken Top and Fall Creek
from Sparks Lake

29 TANGENT TRAILHEAD

STARTING POINT: Drive west from Bend on the Cascade Lakes Highway (Century Drive) #46 for about 13 miles to road #4615 and the Tangent Trailhead sign on the north side of the road. There is limited parking off the road now. It is hoped that in the future there can be provision for more parking here.

ELEVATION: About 5,330' at parking area.

TERRAIN: Very easy roads

MAPS: USDA Forest Service: Deschutes National Forest map
USGS: Wanoga Butte, Oregon, 7.5' 1963 and Broken Top, Oregon 15' 1963

This is a very gentle area of roads where beginers can ski for several miles with almost flat terrain or easy hills. There are open hills to practice turns. This is part of the Swampy Trail System so that there are no dogs or snowmobiles allowed in the area.

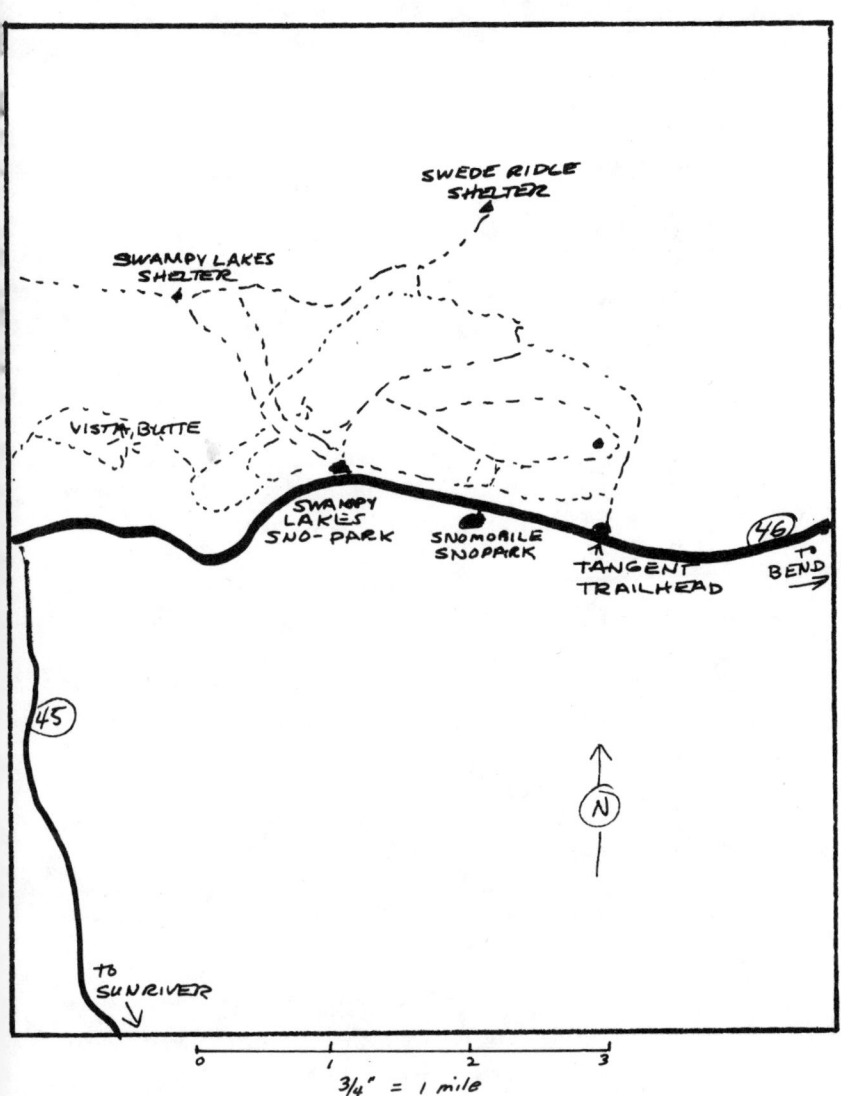

30 TANGENT CHOICES

1. From the parking area go straight up road #4615 (north). At the first junction, keep going straight ahead. This road leads on around the ridge going slowly uphill. After about two miles there is some open space where there is a view of Broken Top and Tam McArthur Rim. If you keep going on this road, it is about 4 miles to Swede Shelter. This is the easiest trail to the shelter.

2. From the parking area go straight up road #4615 to the first junction. Turn left here (Road 4615040). This road leads gradually uphill for about two miles to the Swampy Lakes parking lot. Ski as far as you like as it is a gentle downhill run coming back.

3. TANGENT LOOP: Go straight up road #4615 to the first junction. Turn left and follow this road about two miles to the four-way junction above the Swampy Lakes parking lot. Turn right, going uphill, over the ridge, and downhill to the junction with Road 4615. Go right and follow the road back to the start. This is about a five mile loop.

4. NORDEEN SHELTER: There are several choices for going to Nordeen from Tangent. The closest is to go left on Road 4615040 at the first junction. After about a mile there is a marked trail which takes off up the ridge. Up on the ridge this trail will join the Nordeen Loop. Follow the loop trail to the shelter. Return on the same trail or if it is good snow and you like steep slopes, drop directly down the hill from the shelter to the road.

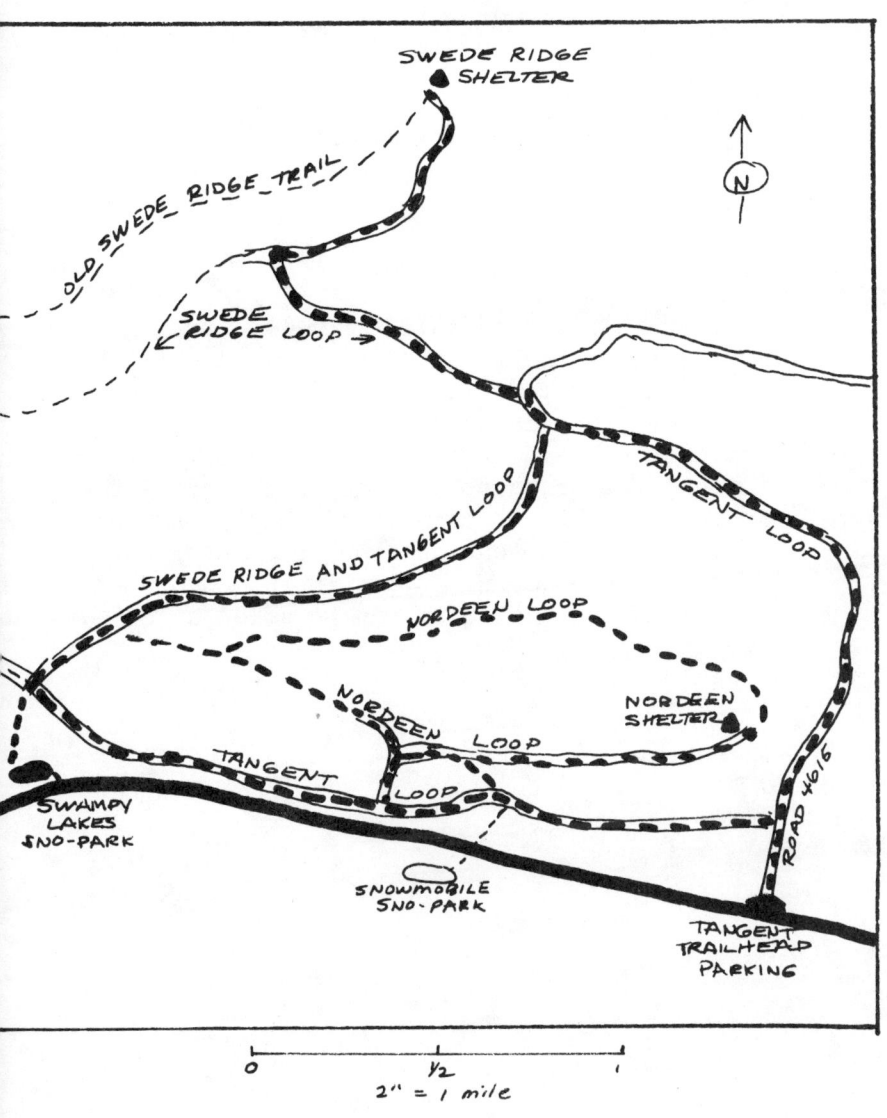

31 TANGENT Practice Hill

Go straight up road #4615 from the parking area. Turn left at the first junction. A short distance up this road (1/4 mile) is a road through the trees (not marked). Watch and you can see the open hillside through the trees. Ski back through the trees to the open slope where there is an excellent area for practicing turns. (Nordeen Shelter can be seen up on top of the ridge.) Another road continues on around to road #4615 so that this can be skied as a short loop. See map.

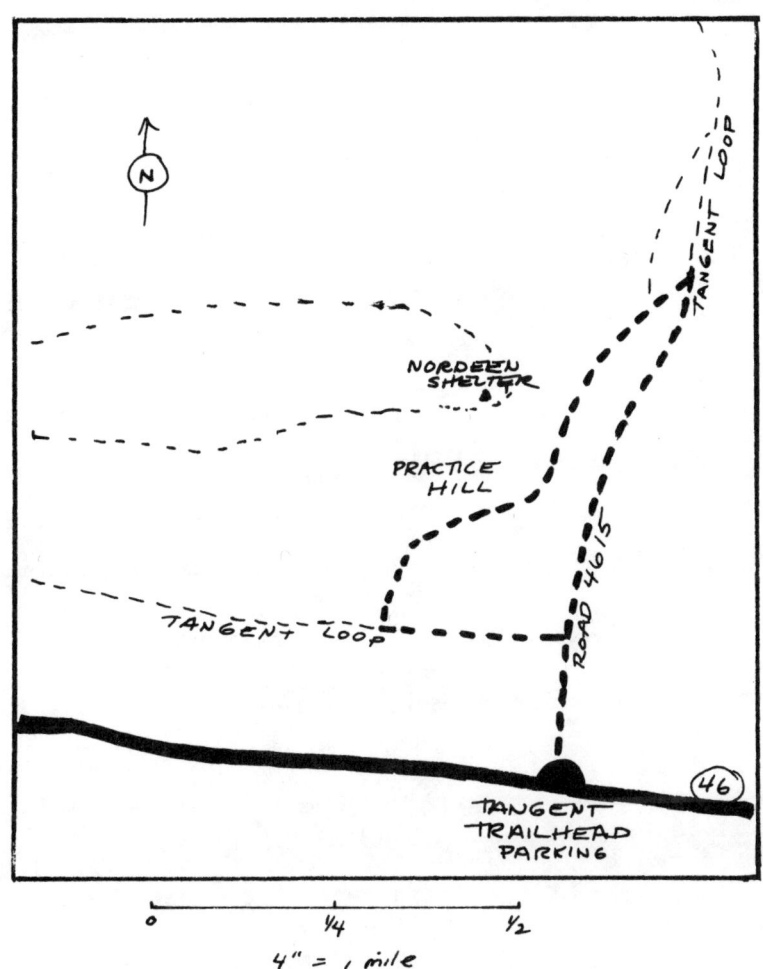

32 BIG SPRING

STARTING POINT: Drive west from Bend on the Cascade Lakes Highway (Century Drive) #46 for about 12 miles. Road #4613 on the south side usually has room for limited parking.

DISTANCE: About 1 1/2 miles to Big Spring

ELEVATION: 5,200' at Big Spring

TERRAIN: Gentle uphill

MAPS: USDA Forest Service: Deschutes National Forest
USGS: Benham Fall, Oregon 7.5' 1963
Wanoga Butte, Oregon 7.5' 1963

The main road you will see in front of you is #4613. This road leads southwest toward Edison Butte and can be skied.

To ski to Big Spring watch for the first road to the right (soon). Once on this little road, it is easy to follow (no marked trail). There are two ways to go on this road. One follows the bottom of the drainage. The other goes along the hillside. Either one is good to ski on. Both come together after about one-half mile. The road seems to end at Big Spring. Explore on your own with a map if you want to go further.

This is a good short trip, near town if you just have a few hours to go out.

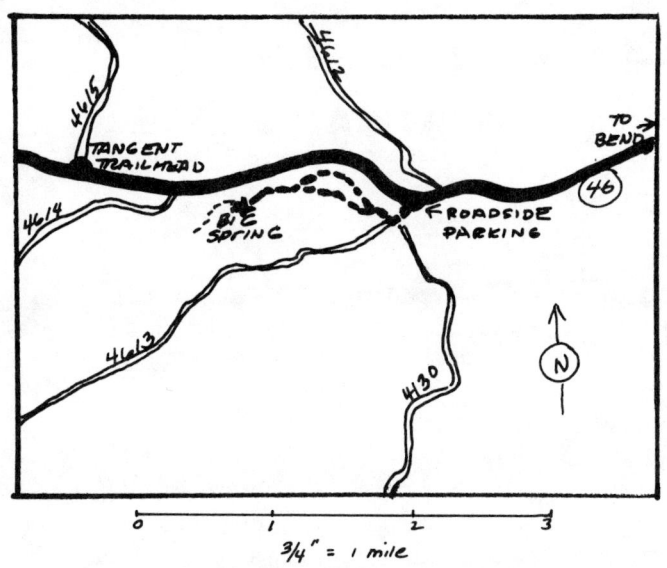

33 KIWA SPRINGS & KIWA BUTTE

From parking at road #4613, follow the main road just a short distance. Road #4130 then goes to the south. It is about three miles to Kiwa Springs. Skiing is easy on gentle terrain with a slight downhill going in.

The springs make a nice lunch stop. If you decide to go further, go west on spur 200 which is the road past the springs. It is about two miles gently uphill to Kiwa Butte.

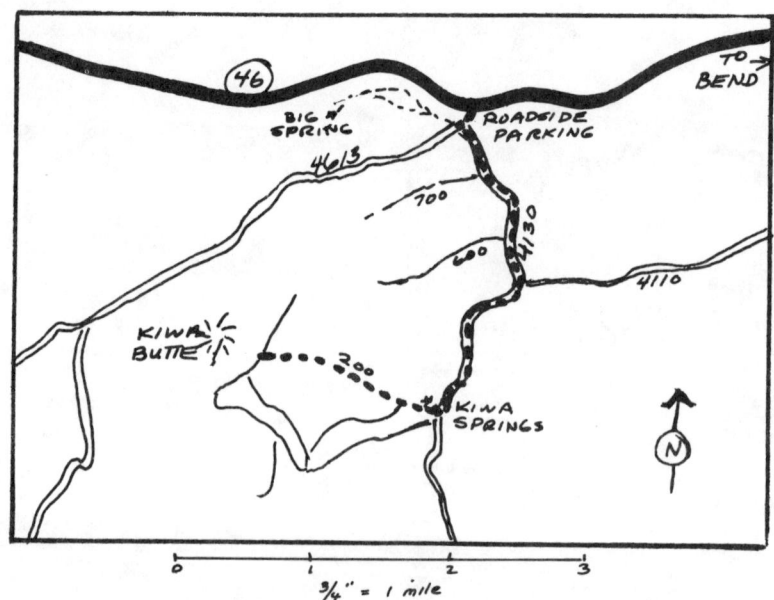

34 KIWA SPRINGS
via road no. 41

Another approach to Kiwi Springs is from road #41. This may only be open if the road is plowed or late in the spring, after snow on the road has melted.

Turn from highway #46 on to road #41 just past the Inn of the Seventh Mountain. About seven miles on this road is road #4130 to the west. Park by the side of the road. Ski trail is not marked but the road is easy to follow. It is uphill until you come to an old corral. The road levels out here and then drops downhill to the springs. In the summer there is a small campground here.

It is about 2 1/2 miles to Kiwa Springs this way.

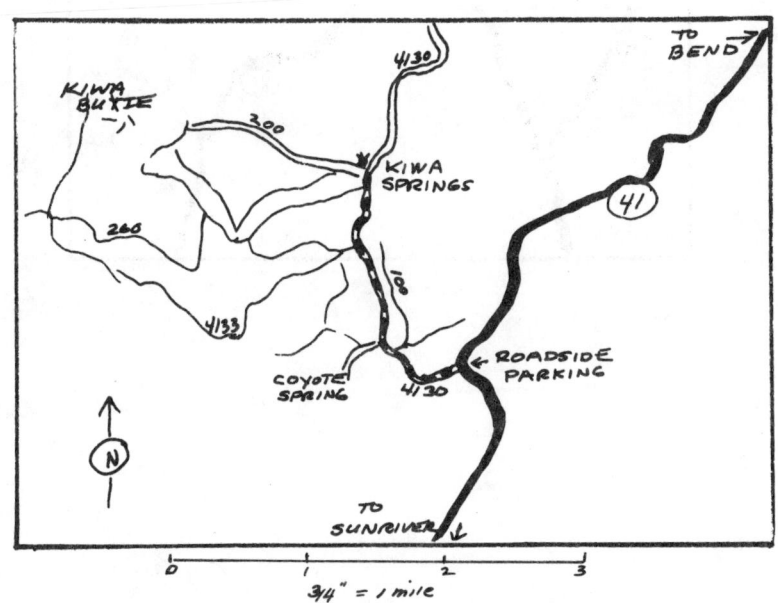

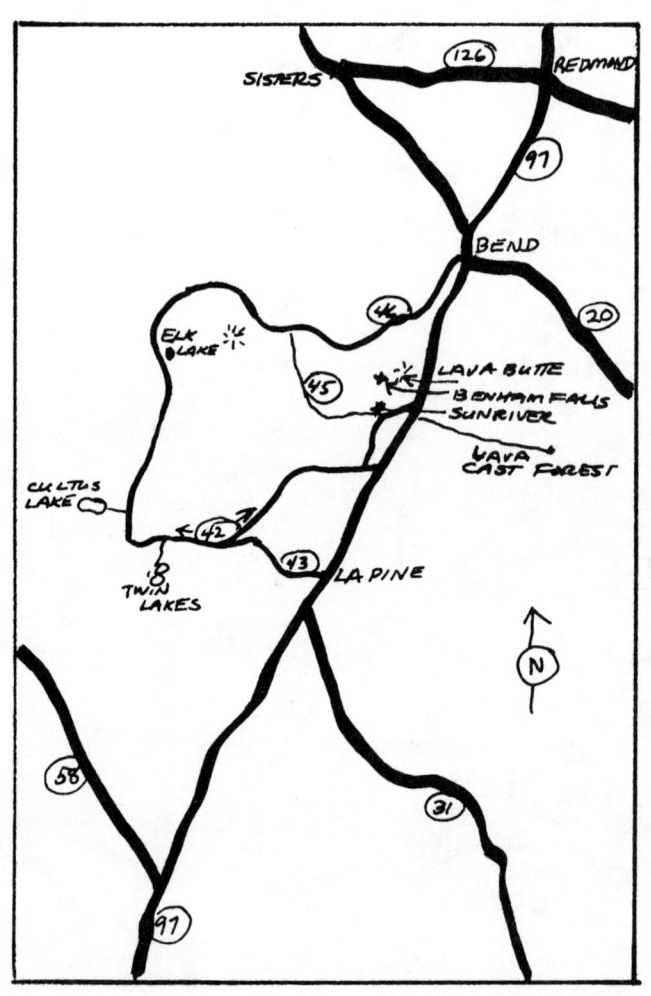

SECTION 2

SOUTH FROM BEND

No.		Page
35.	Lava Butte	70
36.	Benham Falls	71
37.	Lava Cast Forest	72

SUNRIVER TO MT. BACHELOR

38.	Anns Butte	76
39.	Road #4180	78
40.	Junction of Roads #40 & #45	80
41.	Junction of Roads #45 & #4025	82
42.	Edison Ice Cave	84
43.	Dutchman Creek	85

SOUTH CENTURY DRIVE

44.	South Twin Lake	86
45.	Loop around North & South Twin Lakes	88
	Sheep Bridge Campground	88
46.	Cultus Lake	90
47.	Elk Lake from South Century Drive	92

35 LAVA BUTTE

STARTING POINT: Lava Butte is about ten miles south of Bend on Highway #97. Park at the wide turnout by the entrance to Lava Lands Visitor Center.

DISTANCE: One mile to the top of the butte

ELEVATION: Start - 4,502'
Top of Lava Butte - 5,016'

TERRAIN: Fairly steep climb up around the butte. Level at base.

MAPS: USDA Forest Service: Deschutes National Forest
USGS: Lava Butte, Oregon 7.5' 1963

Ski on the main road almost to the Visitor Center. In front of the building the road to the right goes to the butte.

This is level for about 1/2 mile over to the butte. Then the road up the butte is fairly steep. There may be icy spots on the side where the prevailing winds hit Lava Butte. Beautiful view from the top.

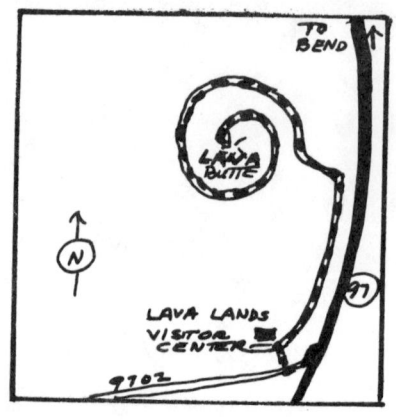

36 BENHAM FALLS

STARTING POINT: Drive south from Bend on highway #97 to the entrance to Lava Lands Visitor Center. There is a wide turnout here where you can park.

DISTANCE: About 4 miles one way
ELEVATION: Parking - about 4,500'
Benham Falls Campground - 4,160'

TERRAIN: Very gentle, easy
MAPS: USDA Forest Service; Deschutes National Forest
USGS: Benham Falls, Oregon 7.5' 1963
Lava Butte, Oregon 7.5' 1963

Start skiing on the road to the Visitor Center. Just past the gate stay to the left on road #9702. This is a good road all the way to the Deschutes River at Benham Falls Campground.

The road gradually drops downhill going in. At the river you can go left into the campground, right up onto the bluff, or cross the bridge and ski another mile on the road down to Benham Falls.

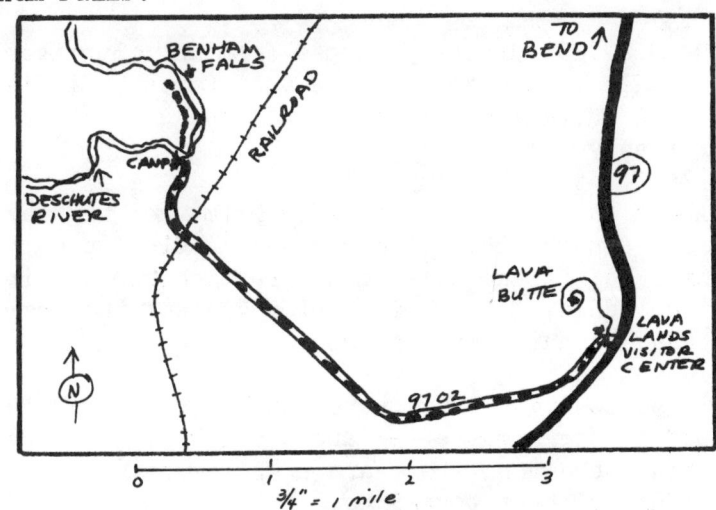

37 LAVA CAST FOREST

STARTING POINT: Drive south from Bend on highway #97 to the main Sunriver junction (40). Park off to the side and out of the way at this junction.

DISTANCE: It is something like 10 or 12 miles to the Lava Cast Forest. This is a good road to ski as far as you want, then go back.

ELEVATION: Cinder Pit - 4,393'
Lava Cast Forest - about 5,200'
Sugar Pine Butte - 5,402'

TERRAIN: Very gentle uphill

MAPS: USDA Forest Service: Deschutes National Forest
USGS: Lava Cast Forest, Oregon 7.6' 1963

Road #9720 directly across from the Sunriver road leads out to the Lava Cast Forest. It is level or very gentle hills all the way. Ski as far as you like.

About one mile up road #9720 from the highway is a cinder pit. It has roads leading up each side of it and some good practice slopes in the middle. There is a nice view of the Cascade Mountains from here.

To go to Sugar Pine Butte watch for road #9724 off to the right after about 5 1/2 miles. By using the map there are a whole network of roads out here to ski on.

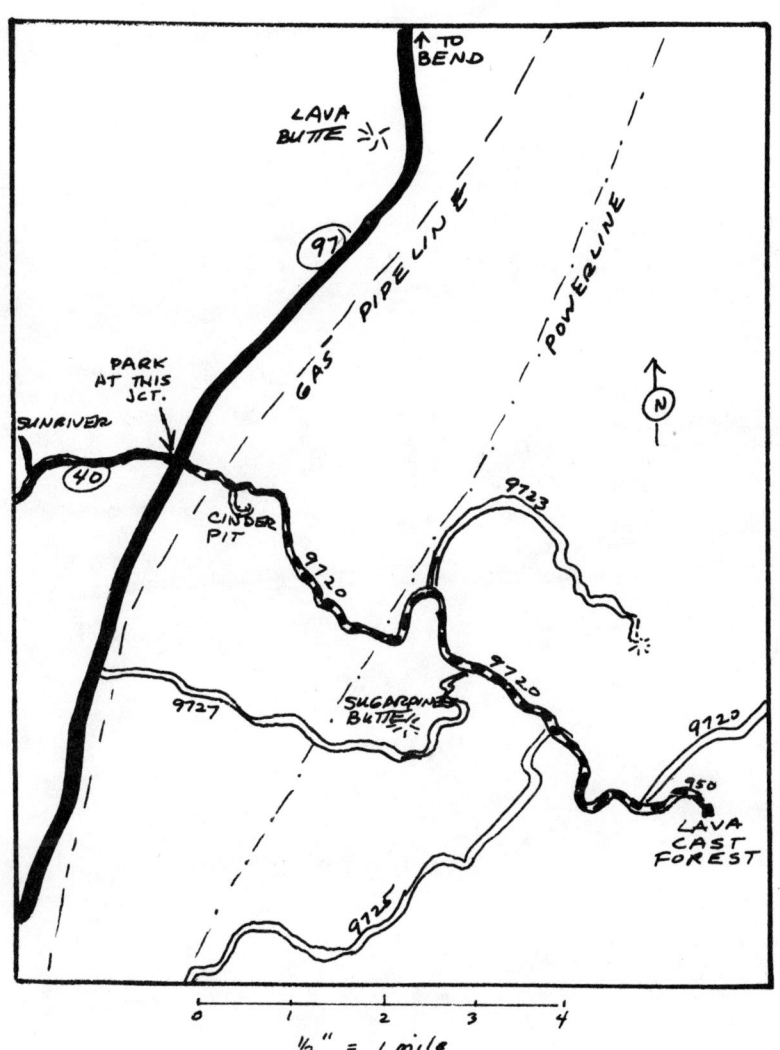

East Lake and Paulina Peak

SUNRIVER - road 45
to MT. BACHELOR

Road #45 was opened for the 1983-84 ski season as a shorter route from Sunriver to Mt. Bachelor.

To reach road #45 go west from Sunriver on road #40 past Spring River. It is about five miles from Sunriver to where road #45 goes to the right.

Along this road are several plowed turn-outs which can be used for parking.

The Sunriver "cut-off" (#45) joins Century Drive several miles below Mt. Bachelor Ski Area.

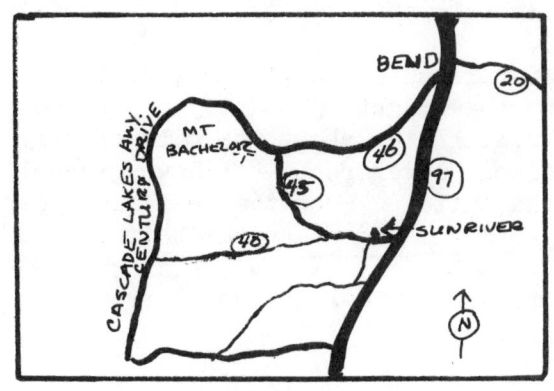

38 ANNS BUTTE

STARTING POINT: Drive south from Bend on highway #97. Then west on Sunriver road #40, past Spring River to the junction with road #41. Park at this junction.

DISTANCE: Cinder pit: 1/2 mile one way
Anns Butte: almost 2 miles one way

ELEVATION: 4,300' at the cinder pit

TERRAIN: Very gentle, except the last 1/2 mile up the butte.

MAPS: USDA Forest Service: Deschutes National Forest
USGS: Anns Butte, Oregon 7.5' 1963
Pistol Butte, Oregon 7.5' 1963

Follow the cinder pit road to the south. It is about 1/2 mile to the cinder pit. This is a good easy practice area with easy slopes for beginning skiers.

The road to Anns Butte (no ski trail markers) goes to the right just as you aproach the cinder pit. After about one mile of very gentle, almost level road, follow gradually around the butte. From the west side there is a spur road which goes up the butte.

There are some views of the surrounding area from the top.

Check with your maps to explore more of the roads near here. They are all nice easy skiing.

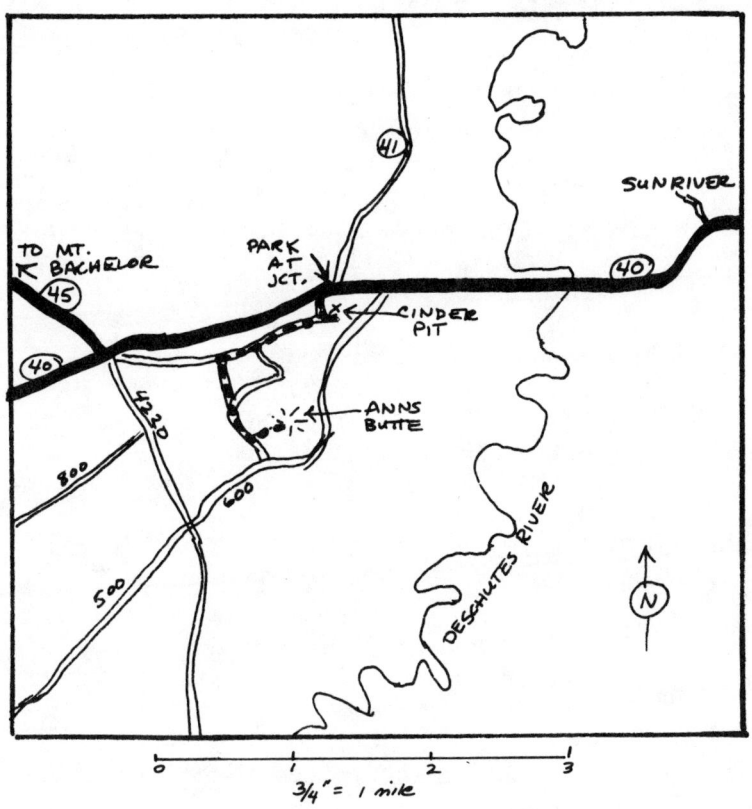

39 ROAD 4180

STARTING POINT: South from Bend on highway #97 Turn on Sunriver road and go past Spring River to road #41 (formerly #1808). If this road is not plowed, ski from here. If possible drive about 1 1/4 miles to the junction of road #4180.

DISTANCE: About 4 miles from the junction of #40 and #41 one way.
About 3 miles to the top of the butte from the junction of #41 and #4180.

ELEVATION: Parking - 4,417'
Top of butte - 4,927'

TERRAIN: Gentle uphill, easy road
Last 1/4 mile up butte is fairly steep.

MAPS: USDA Forest Service: Deschutes National Forest
USGS: Benham Falls, Oregon 7.5' 1963
Wanoga Butte, Oregon 7.5' 1963
Anns Butte, Oregon 7.5' 1963
Pistol Butte, Oregon 7.5' 1963

Follow road #4180 to the west. This is very easy skiing for beginners. After about two miles on the main road there is a junction with road #160. Left on #160 leads you over to and up the little butte which has telephone installations on top. There is a view over Sunriver from here.

If you do not turn on road #160 and stay on road #4180, there is good skiing for several miles on this road. It takes you over toward Pitsua Butte.

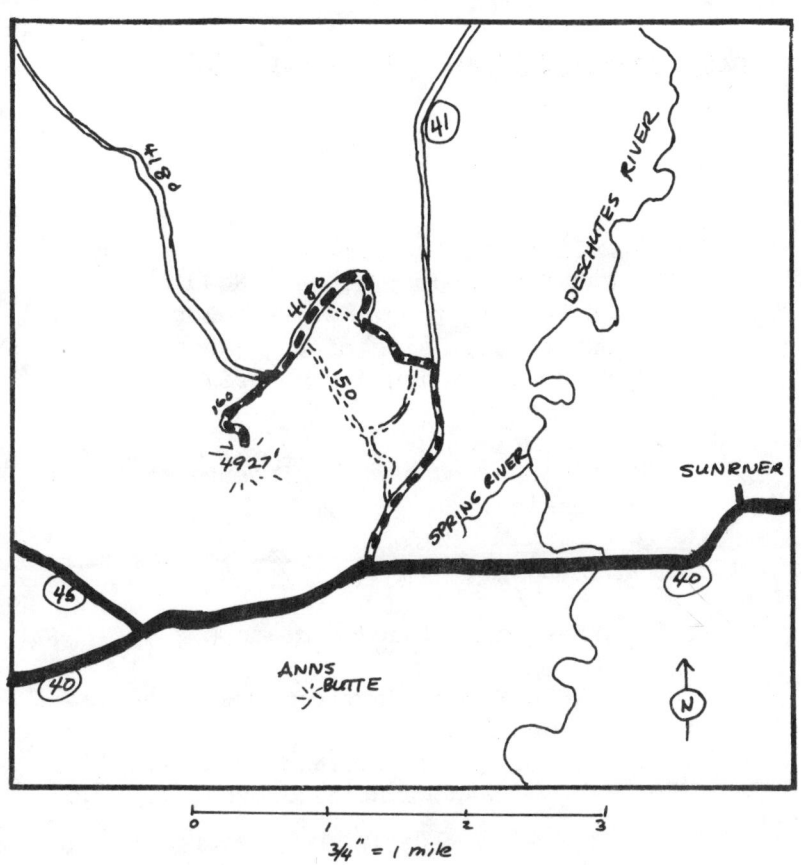

40 JUNCTION of roads 40 & 45

STARTING POINT: West from Sunriver on road #40 for about 5 miles. Road #45 goes to the right to Mt. Bachelor. Park off to the side of the junction, or if road #40 is plowed, drive further west on it.

DISTANCE: Choose roads and distance that you desire.

ELEVATION: About 4,400'

TERRAIN: Easy almost level roads

MAPS: USDA Forest Service: Deschutes National Forest
USGS: Pistol Butte, Oregon, 7.5' 1963
Wanoga Butte, Oregon, 7.5' 1963

From the junction of these two roads there are many forest roads.

Ski on #40 west and then choose #4032 in the vicinity of Sitkum and Pistol Buttes or go on #4030 near Lolo Butte.

Further on out to the west are roads near Lolah Butte and The Three Trappers. Where you ski depends upon how much snow there is and how far the road is plowed.

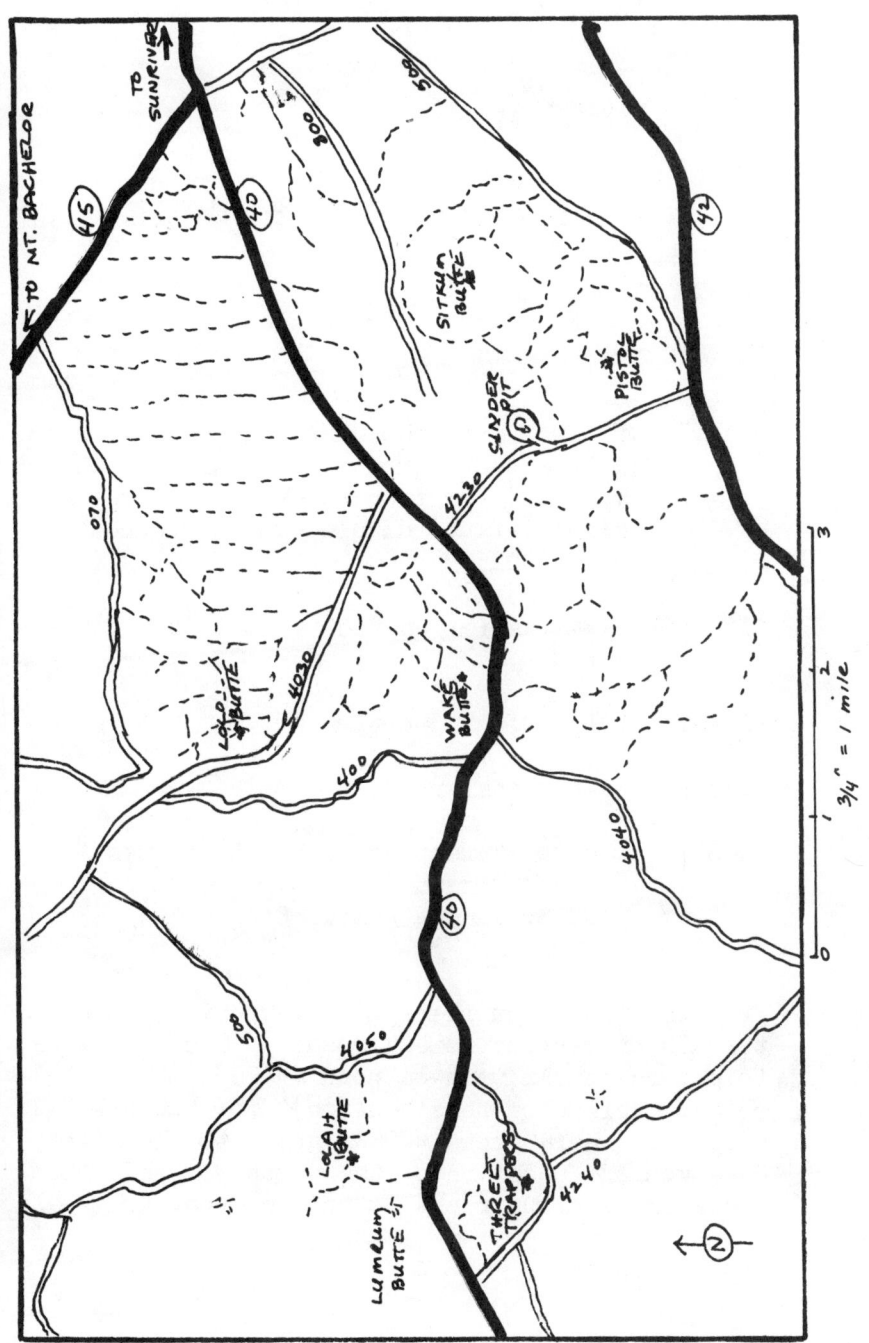

41 JUNCTION

of roads 45 & 4025

STARTING POINT: Go on the Sunriver "cutoff" road #45 either from Century Drive (about 7 miles) or from Sunriver (about 11 miles) to a double plowed turnout at road #4025.

DISTANCE: Ski as far as you want to on forest roads.

ELEVATION: 4,500' at junction

TERRAIN: Very easy roads

MAPS: USDA Forest Service: Deschutes National Forest
USGS: Wanoga Butte, Oregon 7.5' 1963

From this junction there is very nice, gentle terrain on various forest roads. One good area to ski is to ski west on road #4025 (there will be snowmobiles on this section) for about 1/2 mile to where road #200 goes to the right. Once you are back into the woods on this road there are various roads to choose from.

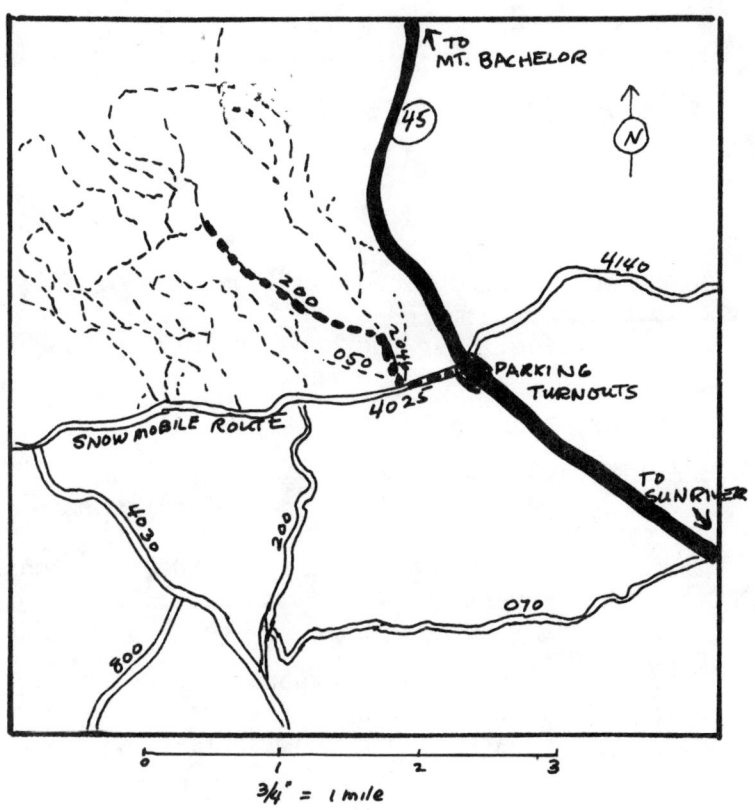

42 EDISON ICE CAVE

STARTING POINT: On road #45 (Sunriver Cutoff) about 5 miles south from Century Drive. Parking here is only if there is a wide place in the road.

DISTANCE: About one mile one way.

ELEVATION: About 4,950'

TERRAIN: Easy road

MAPS: USDA Forest Service: deschutes National Forest
USGS: Wanoga Butte, Oregon 7.5 1963

Edison Ice Cave is an easy trail which is on road #600 most of the way. Skiing here will depend upon parking and snowmobile use.

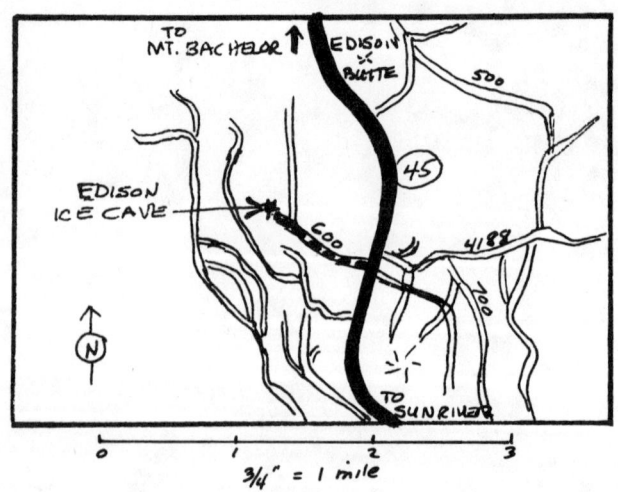

43 DUTCHMAN CREEK
Road 45 just south of Century Drive (46)

STARTING POINT: Road #45 just south of junction with Century Drive #46. There is plowed parking on either side here.

DISTANCE: Choose as far as you like

ELEVATION: About 5,920' at parking

TERRAIN: Gentle open woods
Some roads but mainly just through the woods.

MAPS: USDA Forest Service: Deschutes National Forest
USGS: Wanoga Butte, Oregon 7.5' 1963

There are no marked trails but there is much open country to explore.

To the west of the road (toward Mt. Bachelor) is the best skiing. There is much easy flat skiing from here. You can follow any track which already may be there, or make your own. There is an excellent view of Mt. Bachelor.

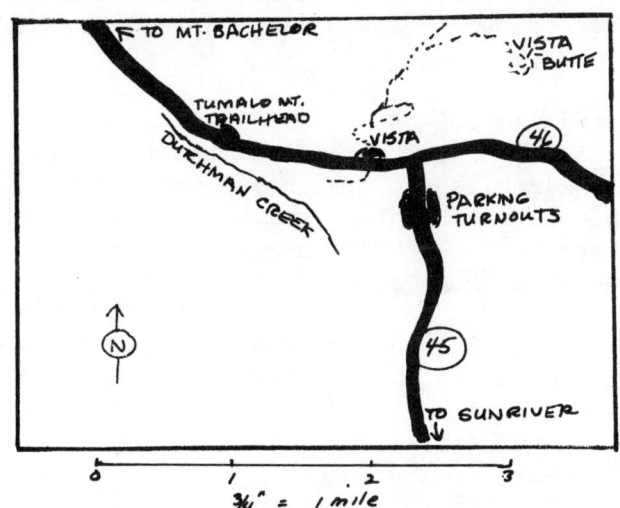

44 SOUTH TWIN LAKE

STARTING POINT: Drive south from Bend on highway #97 to Fall Creek turnoff, #42. Follow road #42 all the way out to Twin Lakes junction (20 miles or so). Turn left on road #4260 for about two miles to parking at South Twin Lake by the resort and campground.

DISTANCE: Gull Point Campground - 1 1/2 miles one way
Wickiup Dam - about 5 miles one way
Loop around North and South Twin Lakes - about 7 miles

ELEVATION: South Twin Lake - 4,430'

TERRAIN: Mostly flat

MAPS: USDA Forest Service: Deschutes National Forest
USGS: Wickiup Dam, Oregon 7.5' 1963
Davis Mt., Oregon 7.5' 1963

GULL POINT: Ski on road #4260 on beyond South Twin Lake. This road is not plowed. It is about 1 1/2 miles to Gull Point Campground. Ski around the roads in the campground for views of the part of Wickiup Reservoir where the Deschutes River runs into it.

WICKIUP DAM: Continue on road #4260 on past Gull Point Campground. The road from here out to Wickiup Dam is very straight and very flat. From here, the view is of Davis Mt. and other buttes in the area.

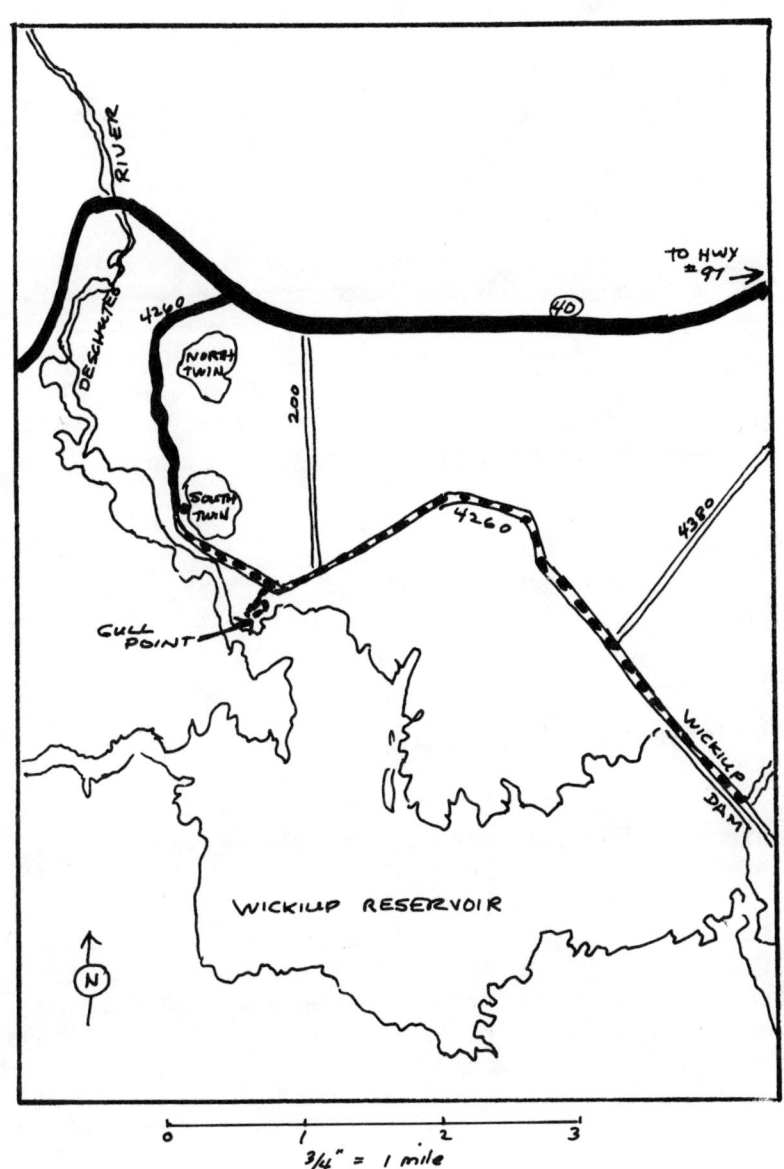

45 loop around
NORTH & SOUTH TWIN LAKES

Ski on road #4260 a short distance beyond Gull Point Campground to the junction with road #4262. Turn left on road #4262. This road goes straight north for almost two miles. When you reach road #42, you can follow it and road #4260, south and back to Twin Lakes, or there are some side roads in the area to explore.

SHEEP BRIDGE C.G.

This is in the area on the west side of road #4260 and north of Twin Lakes Campgrounds. Go across the road (west) from the resort to the Deschutes River. There is no definite road or trail from here but the woods are open enough that you can ski on bits of road and open woods all the way along the river for about 1 1/2 miles to Sheep Bridge Campground.

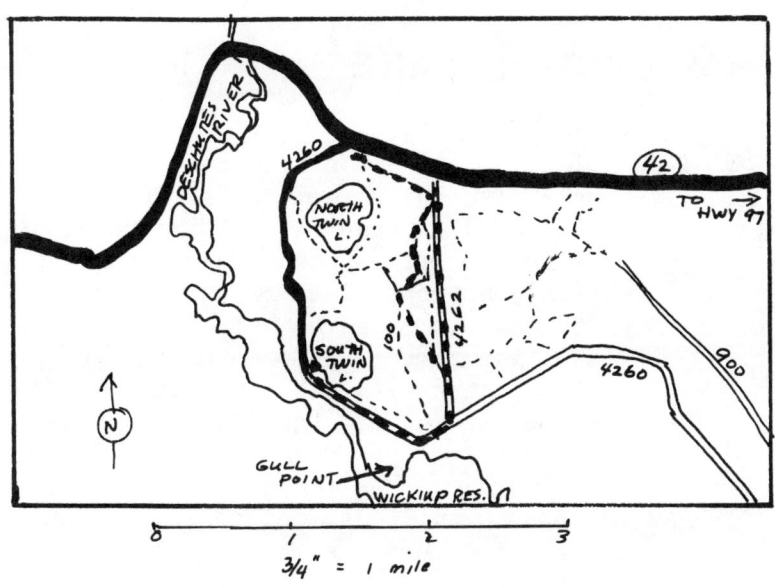

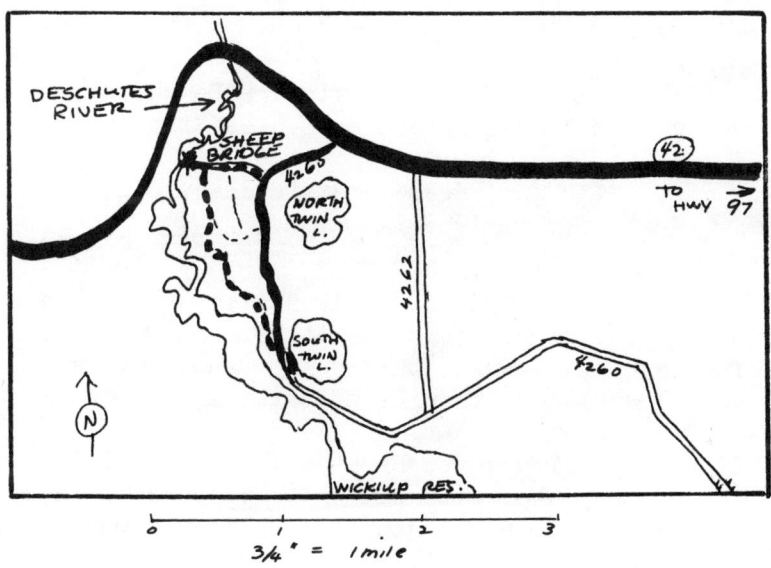

46 CULTUS LAKE

STARTING POINT: Drive south from Bend on highway #97 to Fall Creek turn off, road #42. Follow road #42 all the way out to Century Drive (road #46) past Twin Lakes junction. Turn right (north) on #46 for six or seven miles to Cultus Lake junction. Before making this trip, check with the county or Forest Service to see if the road is plowed this far.

DISTANCE: About 2 miles to end of campground, as far around the lake as you wish from there.

ELEVATION: Cultus Lake - 4,668'

TERRAIN: Almost flat

MAPS: USDA Forest Service: Deschutes National Forest and Three Sisters Wilderness
USGS: Crane Prairie Reservoir, Ore. 7.5' 1963
Irish Mt., Oregon 7.5' 1963

Ski on road #4635 to Cultus Lake Campground. Ski on the road if it hasn't been plowed. If it has been plowed, there is usually room to ski along the north side of the road.

At the campground you have the option to ski on around the lake. (DO NOT ski across the lake.) You can continue along the shoreline or back in the woods near the hiking trail.

Cultus Lake is the starting point for skiing cross country to Muskrat Lake where there is a historic log cabin. This old cabin is kept in usable condition by volunteer skiers and hikers.

Along the road to Cultus Lake

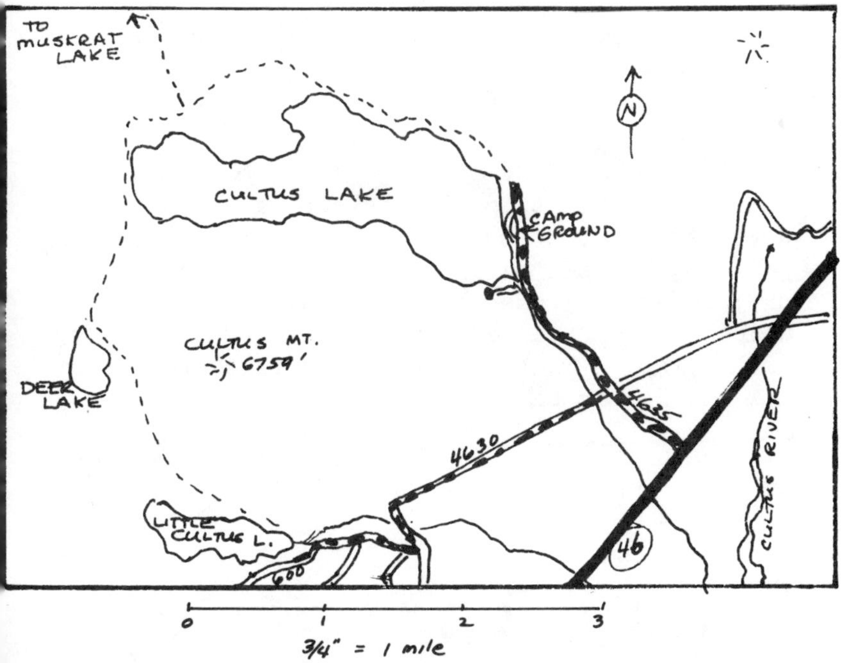

47 ELK LAKE

from south Century Drive (46)

STARTING POINT: Follow directions to Cultus Lake. From there continue north as far as the road is plowed.

DISTANCE: This will vary greatly, depending upon how far you can drive.

ELEVATION: Elk Lake - about 4,880'

TERRAIN: Almost level, gentle rolling hills

MAPS: USDA Forest Service: Deschutes National Forest
USGS: Elk Lake, Oregon 7.5' 1963

This is a nice trip in the spring after they have started to plow the road. Drive as far as you can, then ski on the road to Elk Lake. There are also side roads to explore and other lakes which can be reached by going cross country with a map. There are nice mountain views from Elk and Hosmer Lakes.

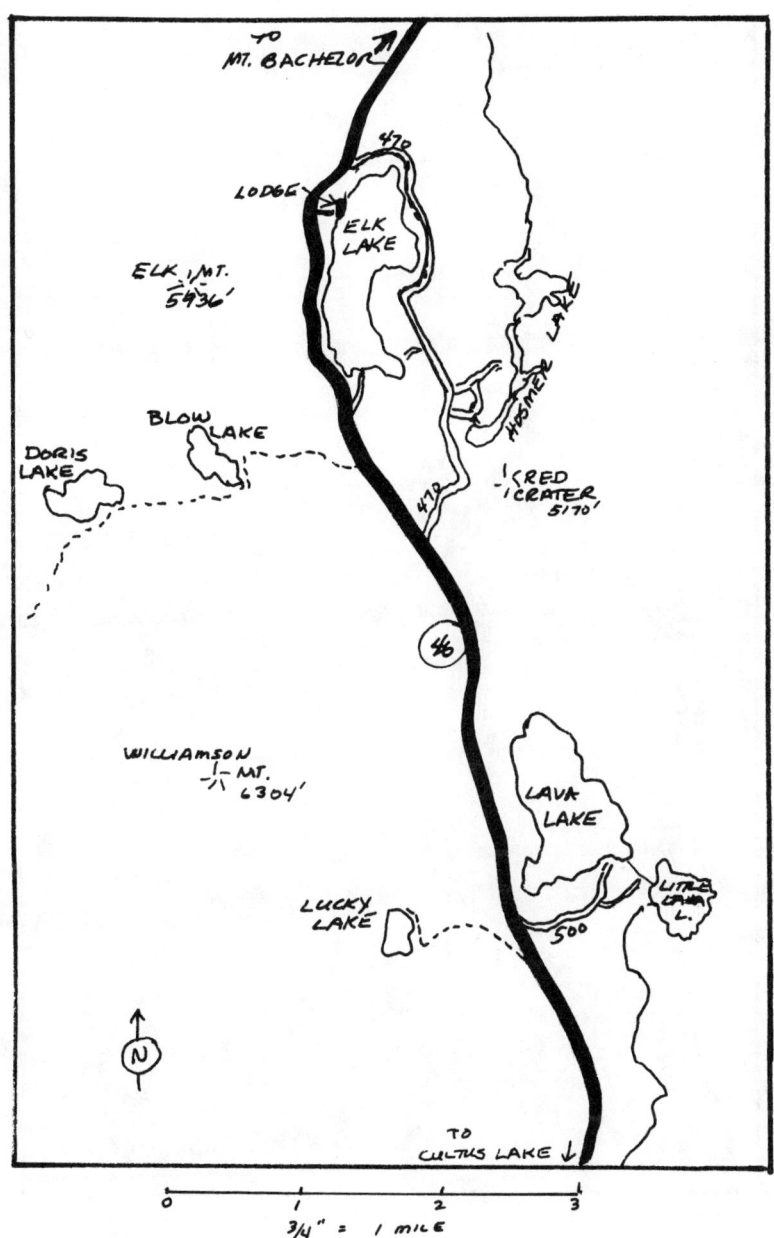

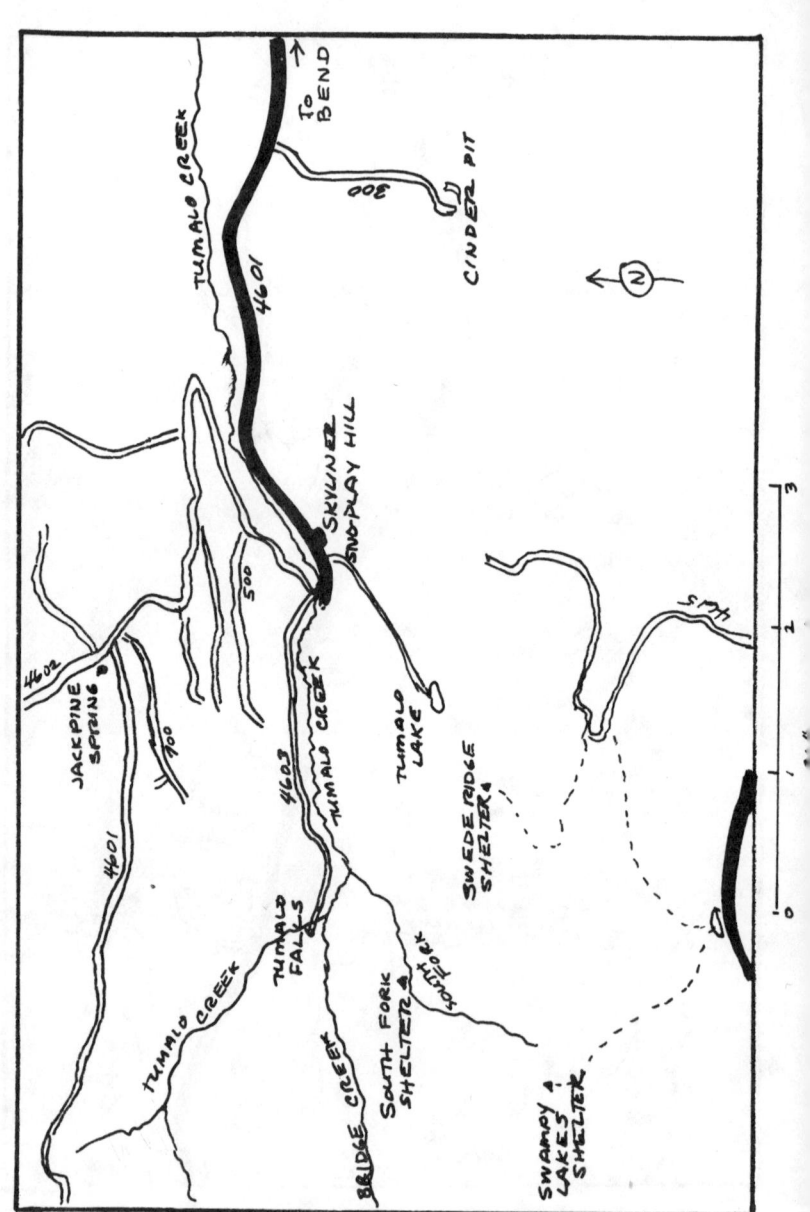

SECTION 3

SKYLINER ROAD & TUMALO FALLS

No.		Page
48.	Cinder Pit - Skyliner Road	96
49.	Skyliner - Snowplay Area	98
50.	Tumalo Falls	100
51.	South Fork Shelter	103
52.	Cougar Ridge	104
53.	Jackpine Spring	104

48 CINDER PIT - SKYLINER ROAD

STARTING POINT: Drive west from Bend on Galveston Street. As you leave town this street becomes Skyliner Road. This is the main paved road to Tumalo Falls (#4601). About six or seven miles from town, watch for road #300 on the left. Park along the highway off to the side of the road.

DISTANCE: About 1 1/2 miles one way. 3 miles round trip.

ELEVATION: About 4,600'

TERRAIN: Easy, very moderate hills

MAPS: USDA Forest Service: Deschutes National Forest
USGS: Broken Top, Oregon 15' 1959

Follow road #300 south from the highway. There are gentle rolling hills, but nothing very steep. This main road leads right to the cinder pit. There are also side roads to be followed.

At the cinder pit are a variety of open hills to practice skiing on. Beyond the cinder pit are some other roads leading on through the woods if the snow is deep enough.

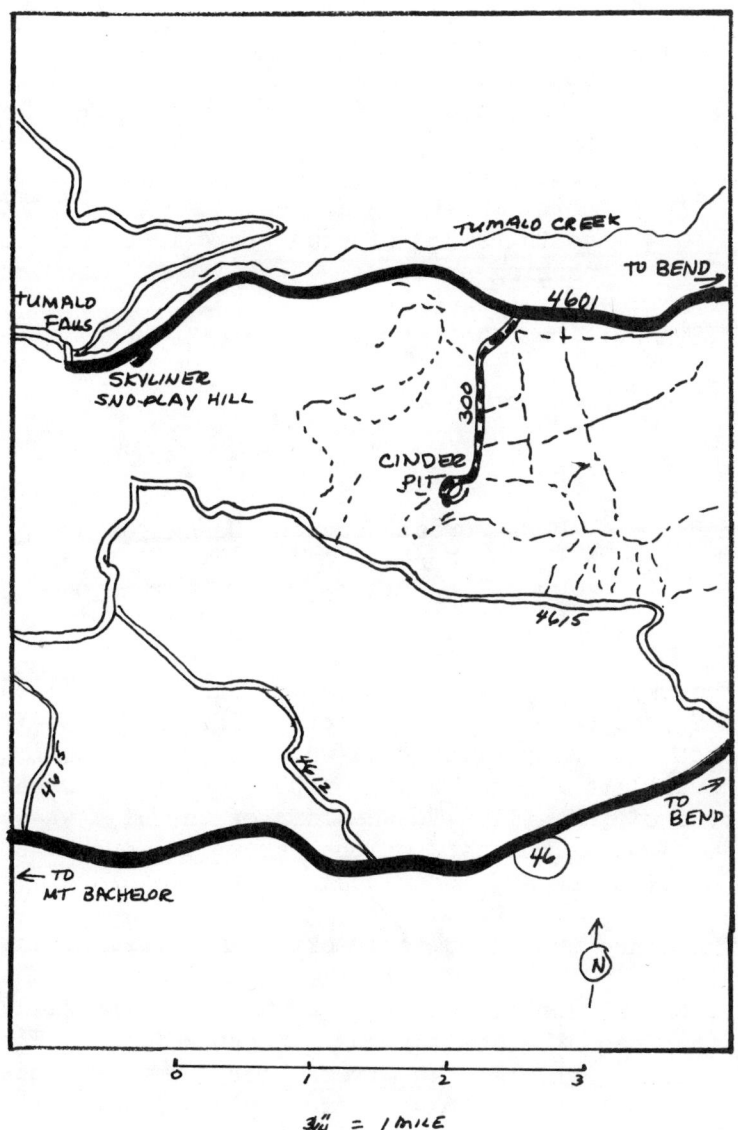

49 SKYLINER snow play area

STARTING POINT: Drive west from Bend on Galveston Street. As you leave town this street becomes Skyliner Road. This is the main paved road to Tumalo Falls (road #4601). About nine miles from town (past the houses) on the left, south side of the road is a plowed parking area.

DISTANCE: Two short trails, one mile each

ELEVATION: About 4,800'

TERRAIN: Easy

MAPS: USDA Forest Service: Deschutes National Forest
USGS: Broken Top, Oregon 15' 1959

The Skyliner snow-play area was Bend's original ski area before Mt. Bachelor. The hill just in front of the parking area was cleared for skiing downhill. There was a rope tow up the right side of the hill. To the left of the hill was a ski jump. This part of the area is much used for sledding and inner-tubing now.

There are two short, easy ski trails from here:

1. One starts to the right as you face the hill. Go past the shelter and across a flat. The trail enters the trees here, however this area is being logged, so you may have to ski for a ways before finding where the trail enters the trees. This is a narrow little trail where the trees are close on either side. This makes it a really pretty trail just after a new snow storm. This trail leads to the old "Skyliner Lodge".

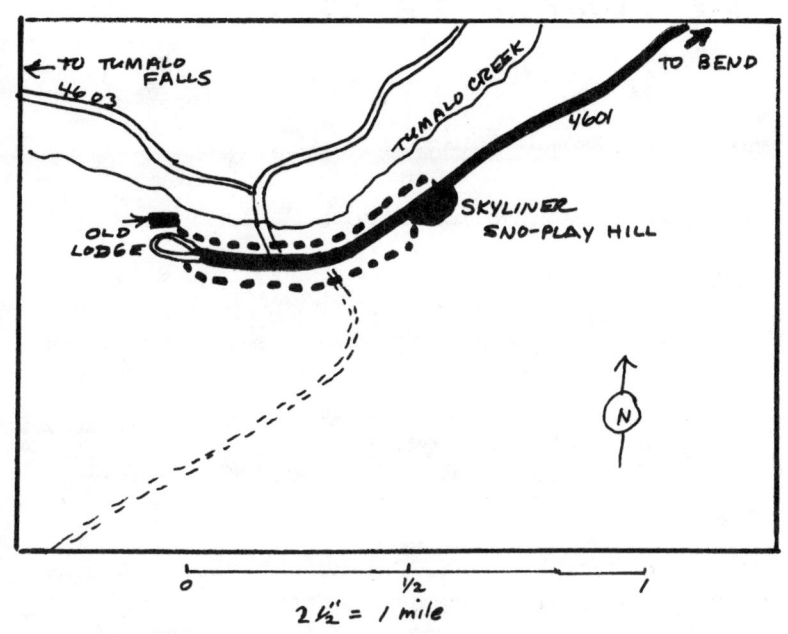

2. The other short, little trail is across the road from the parking lot. It is between the road and Tumalo Creek. Enter the trees across from the parking area and you will see the power lines. Follow the power lines. This trail can be used as an access to the bridge and the road to Tumalo Falls.

50 TUMALO FALLS

STARTING POINT: Skyliner snow-play area

DISTANCE: About 6 miles round trip

ELEVATION: 4,800'

TERRAIN: Almost level, very easy

MAPS: USDA Forest Service: Deschutes National Forest
USGS: Broken Top, Oregon 15' 1959

From the parking area, follow the road, or the power line trail across the road, 1/4 mile to where road #4601 turns downhill to the right and crosses Tumalo Creek. Just across the bridge is a gate and a road to the left. Go around the gate and follow the road. It is about three miles to the falls.

This is the area of the Bridge Creek fire of July, 1979. If the snow is deep enough, the open slopes of the fire offer good skiing.

Tumalo Falls is to the right after crossing the bridge at the picnic area. Just above here on Bridge Creek is a Bend city water intake.

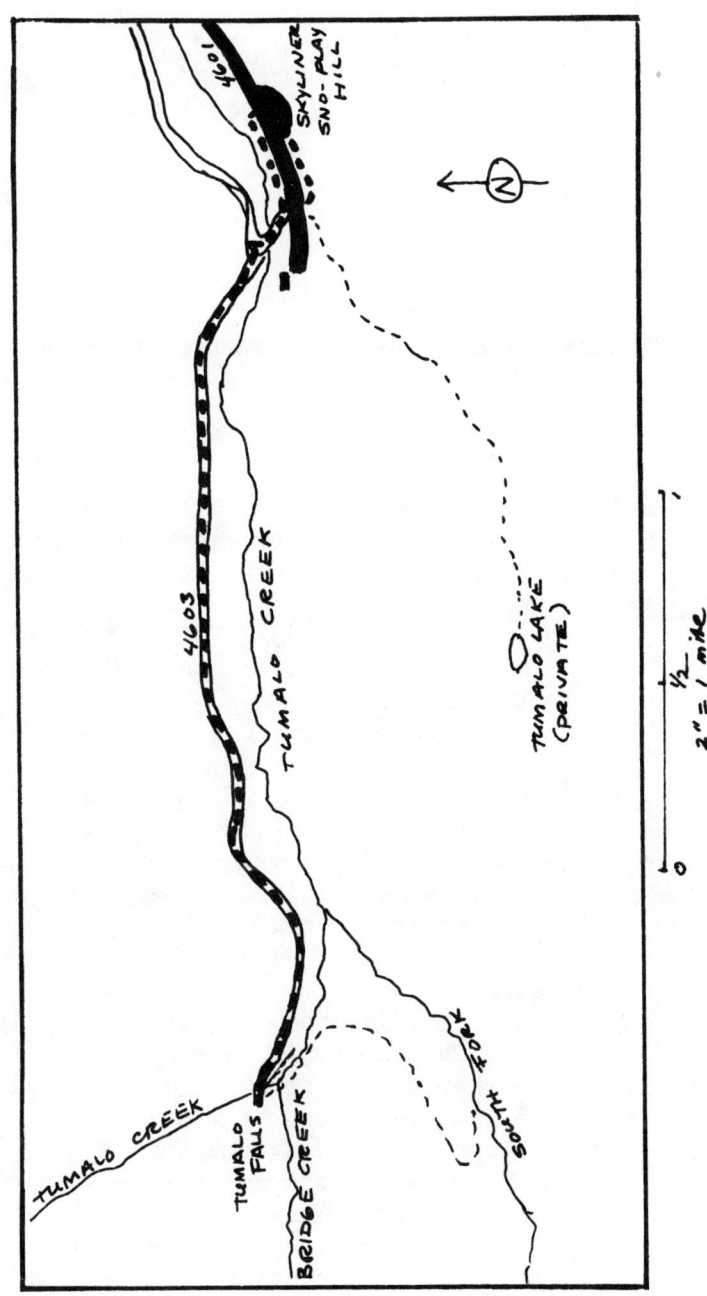

51 SOUTH FORK SHELTER

STARTING POINT: Ski to Tumalo Falls, parking at Skyliner snow-play area.

DISTANCE: About 8 miles round trip from Skyliner parking

ELEVATION: 4,800' to 5,000'

TERRAIN: Almost level. Easy except for the last 1/2 mile before the shelter. This is through the trees and is more difficult.

MAPS: USDA Forest Service: Deschutes National Forest
USGS: Broken Top, Oregon 15' 1969

Follow the directions for skiing to Tumalo Falls. After crossing the bridge over Tumalo Creek, at the picnic area, the ski trail goes sharply to the left just across the bridge.

A short distance down-stream is a small bridge which crosses Bridge Creek. Cross the bridge and go left. The ski trail crosses the burned area to the trees on the south. Just back into the trees is the south fork of Tumalo Creek. If snow conditions are good you can ski on the side of the creek to the shelter (about 1/2 mile). Another route is to the right after crossing the burned area. Go up the hill on the ridge where there is a cleared ski trail on the side hill. This goes above the shelter and circles back down the hill to the shelter.

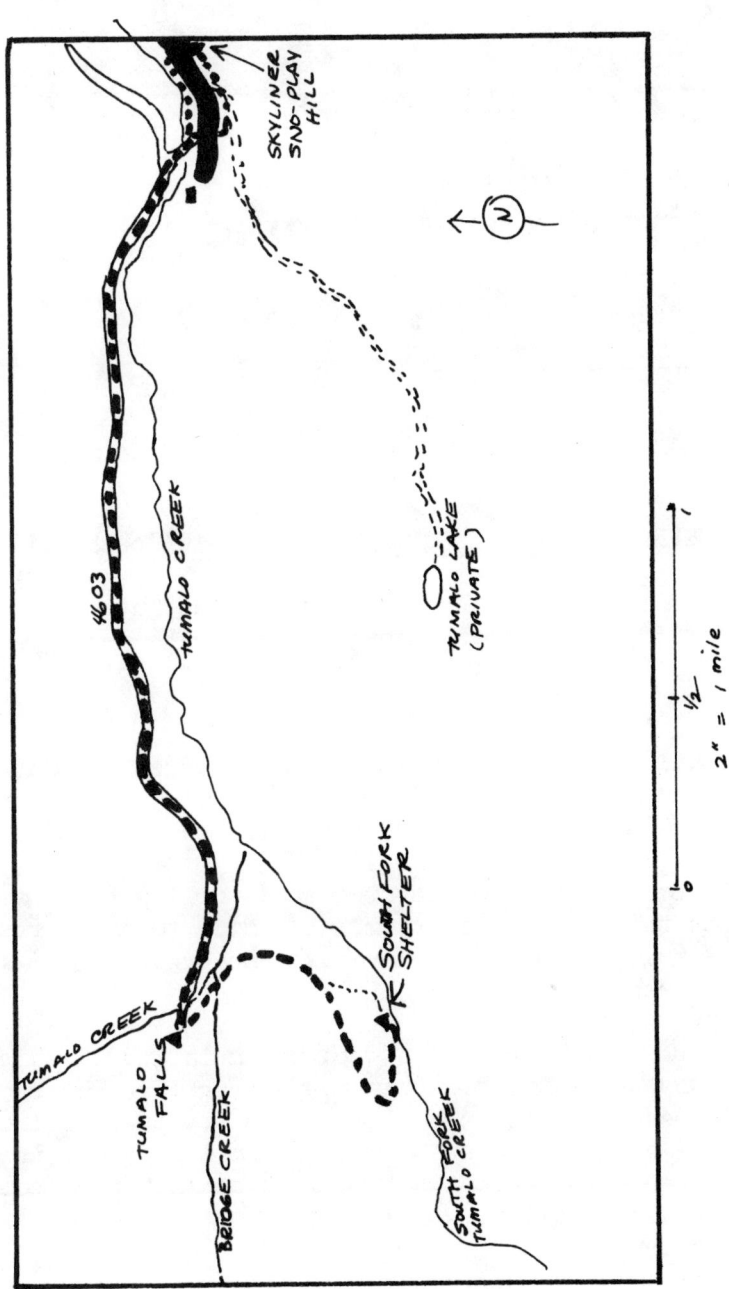

52 COUGAR RIDGE
and
53 JACKPINE SPRING

STARTING POINT: Skyliner snow-play area

DISTANCE: About 5 miles one way

ELEVATION: Skyliner 4,800'
     Top of ridge

TERRAIN: Uphill going in, downhill back out

MAPS: USDA Forest Service: Deschutes National Forest
USGS: Broken Top, Oregon, 15' 1959

Skiing up road #4601 to Cougar Ridge and Jackpine Spring will be good only if there is enough snow that cars cannot drive on the road.

From the Skyliner parking area follow the road, or the power line trail, 1/4 mile to where road #4601 turns right downhill and crosses Tumalo Creek.

Across the creek stay on the main road, which goes uphill and curves to the right. The road is easy for about a mile, then starts to climb the ridge. After about two miles there is a sharp switch-back to the left as the road continues to climb. The view from the top is excellent.

Jackpine Spring is beyond the top of the ridge, after the road levels out and goes to the right. The spring is a short distance on road #4602.

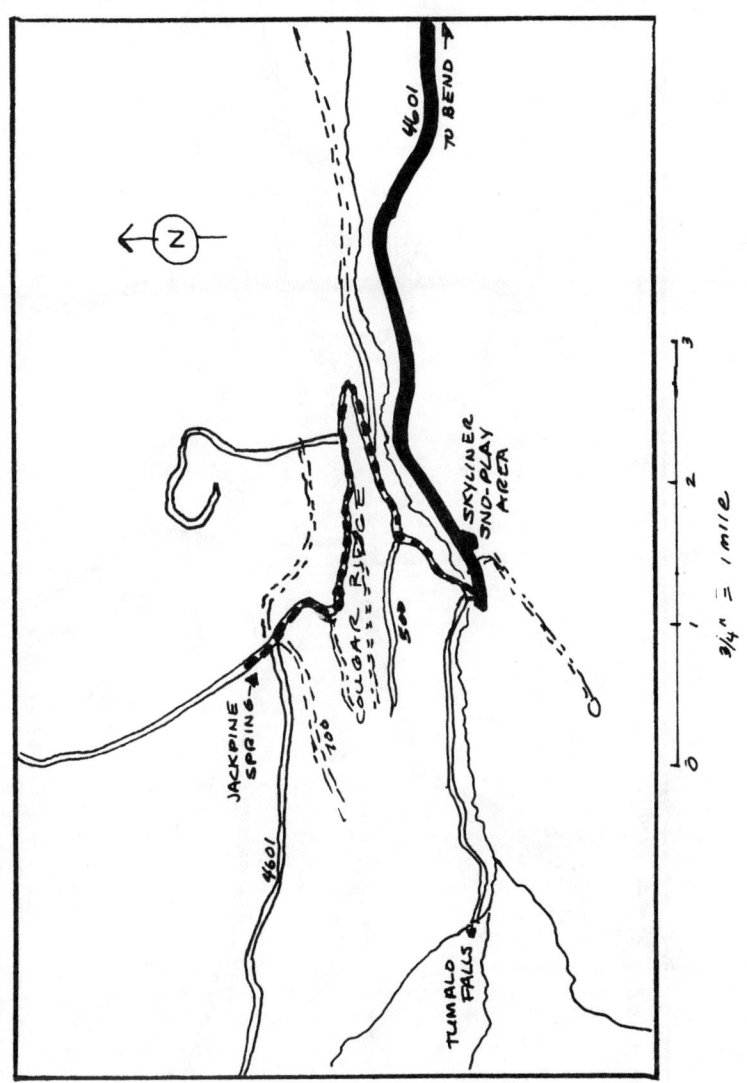

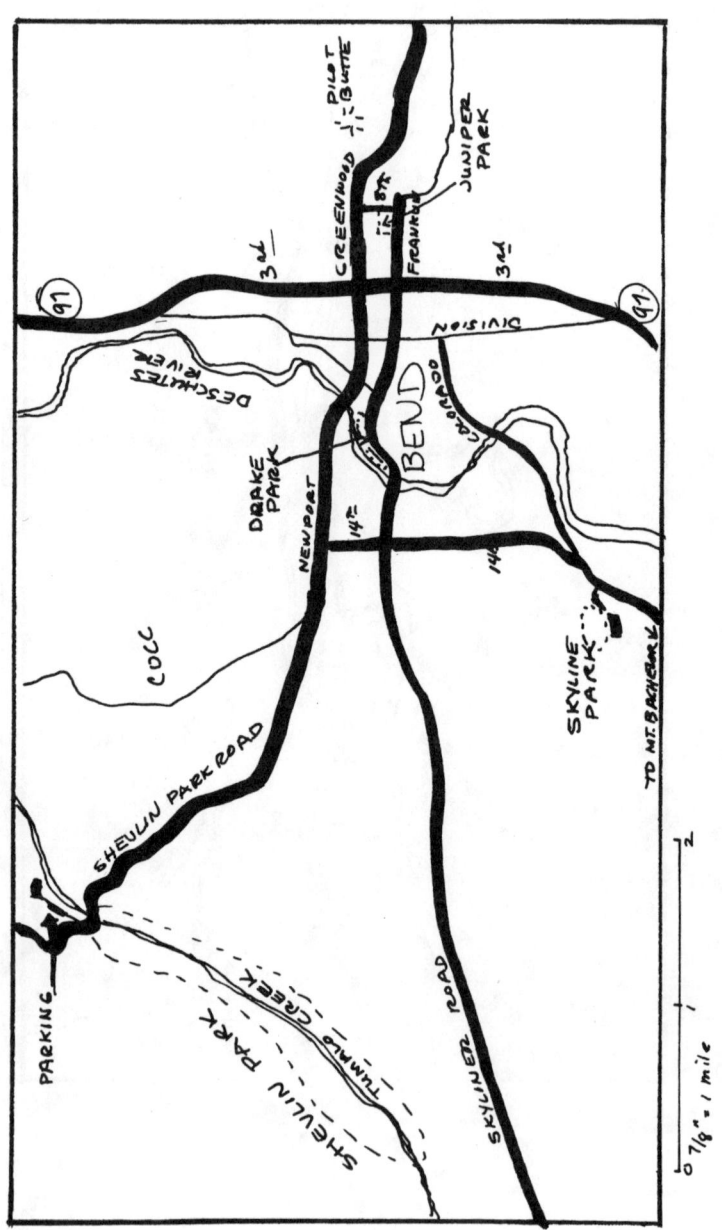

SECTION 4

IN OR NEAR BEND

No.		Page
54.	Shevlin Park	108
55.	Skyline Park	110
56.	Drake Park	111
57.	Juniper Park	111

58 SHEVLIN PARK

STARTING POINT: Drive west from Bend on Newport Street. At the edge of town, Newport Street becomes Shevlin Park Road. It is about 5 miles to the park. There is parking at Shevlin Park Hatchery, to the right shortly across the bridge over Tumalo Creek.

DISTANCE: About 1 1/2 miles to the end of the park.

ELEVATION: 3,600'

TERRAIN: almost level

MAPS: USDA Forest Service; Deschutes National Forest
USGS: Shevlin Park, Oregon 7.5' 1962

Shevlin Park is a City of Bend park with many year round activities.

To start skiing, cross the road from the hatchery. Start skiing by the gate up the main road. If the snow is not very deep it is best to ski on the road. With deeper snow it is possible to ski over along Tumalo Creek on the various roads around through the park.

The main road leads the length of the park up to Freemont Meadow. This is close to town and is very easy skiing.

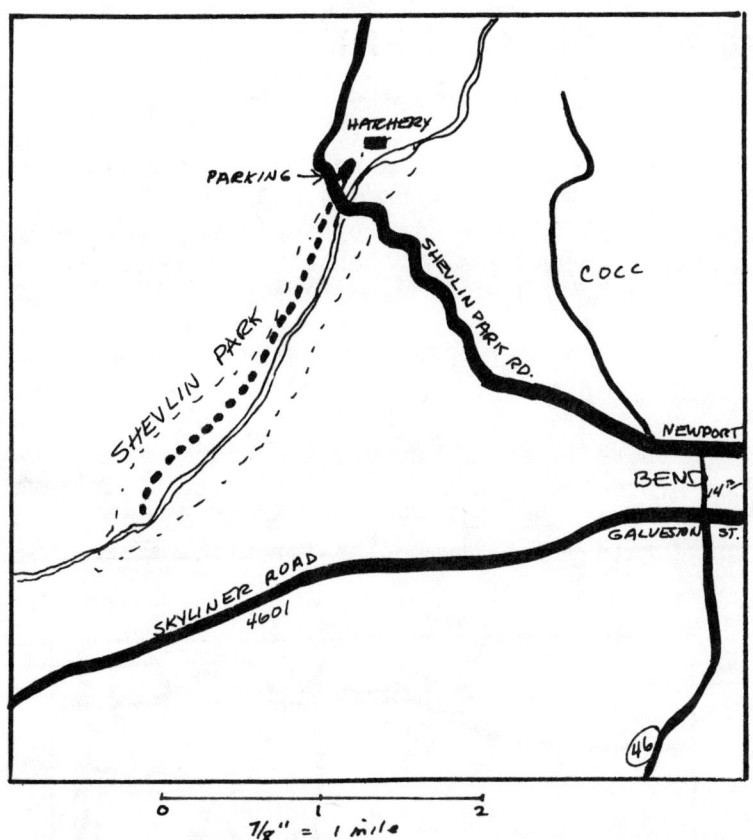

55 SKYLINE PARK

To reach Skyline Park, drive out either Colorado Street or 14th Street to where Century Drive begins. Skyline Park is by Cascade Junior High School (behind the Mt. Bachelor car pool parking lot).

This park is administered by Bend Parks and Recreation Department.

When there is enough snow, this park sometimes has groomed cross country trails or will have trails that are skied out. When skiing is good the lights may be turned on for night skiing.

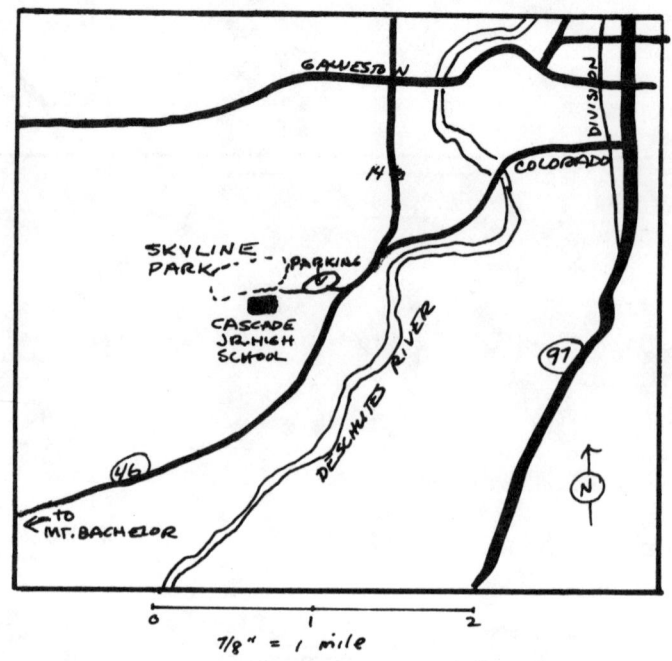

56 DRAKE PARK

Drake Park is near downtown Bend, along the Deschutes River. It is a long, fairly narrow park, allowing for ski trails which can be used for training. If there is enough snow there are usually cross country trails around the park. Some light from street lights and park lights make night skiing possible. Parking can be either in the Mirror Pond parking lot or along Riverside Boulevard.

57 JUNIPER PARK

Juniper Park can be reached by parking by 7th and Franklin Streets by the tennis courts, or by parking near the swimming pool off of 6th Street. Juniper Park is big enough for a large loop trail to be made. By the tennis courts and by the swimming pool there are little hills to practice on.

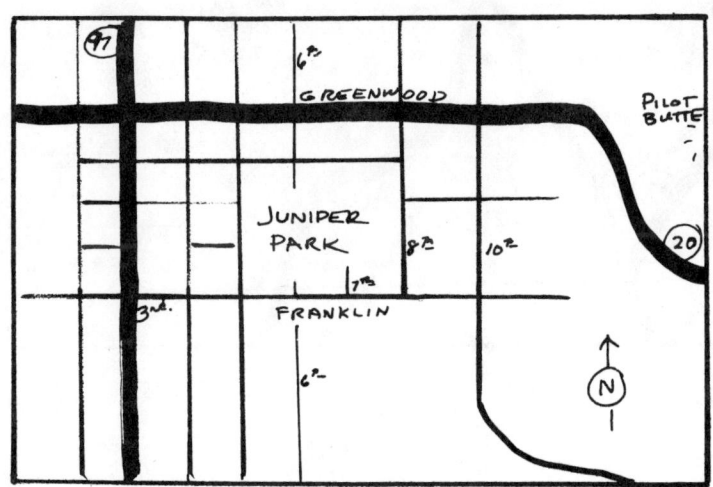

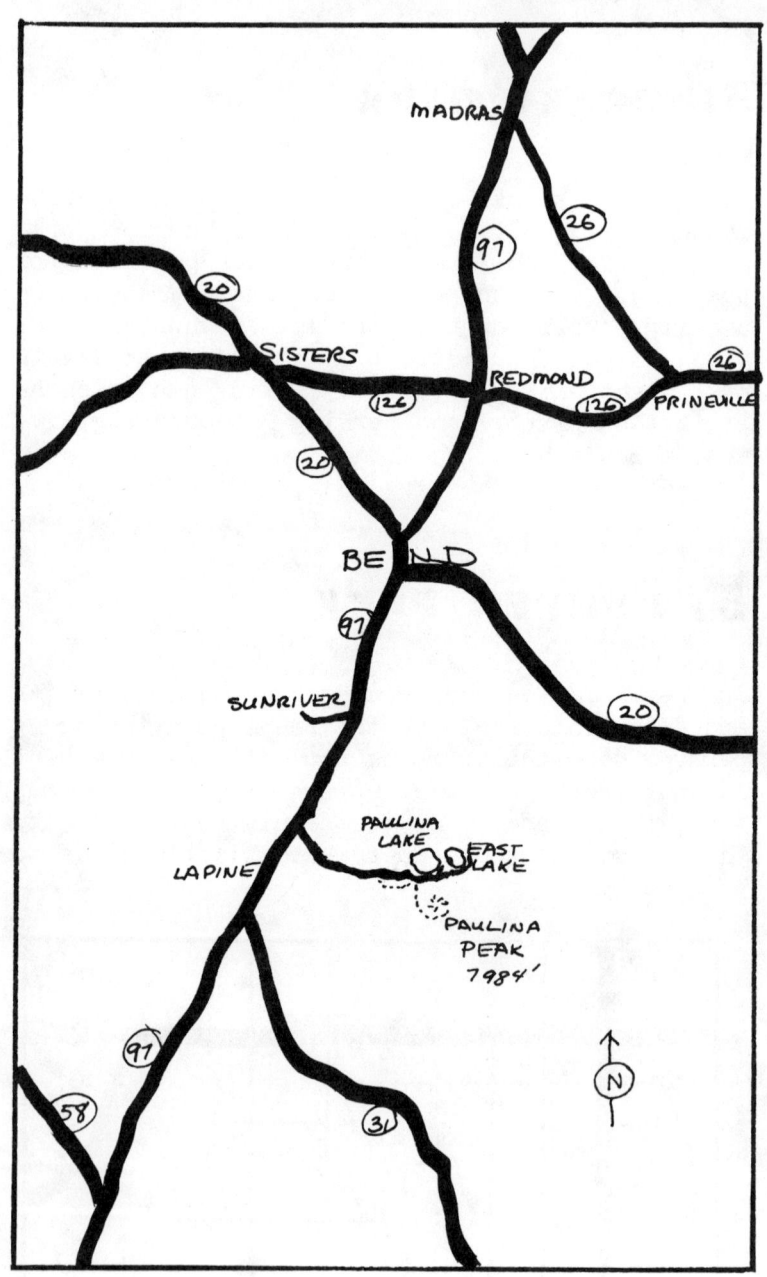

Paulina Peak and the ski trail to Paulina Lake

SECTION 5

NEWBERRY CRATER

No.		Page
58.	Paulina Lake Trail	114
59.	Paulina Peak	116
60.	Little Crater Campground	118
61.	East Lake	119

58 PAULINA LAKE

STARTING POINT: Drive south from Bend on Highway #97 to the Paulina-East Lake junction (road #21). Turn left to the east on this road. The sno-park which is the start of the ski trail is about ten miles after you turn on to raod #21.

DISTANCE: 3 1/2 miles one way, 7 miles round trip.
ELEVATION: At the sno park - 5,600'
Paulina Lake - 6,331'

TERRAIN: Moderate uphill going in, downhill coming out.

MAPS: USDA Forest Service: Deschutes National Forest
USGS: Paulina Peak, Oregon, 7.5'1963

This is a newly marked cross country ski trail. It is nice because it is closed to snowmobiles. This trail means that skiers no longer have to ski up the highway.

The trail begins to the right just before the snow gate. Look for ski trail markers down into the trees. The trail then curves to the left into the trees along the edge of an open logged area.

After crossing a logging road, the ski trail is well marked as it follows uphill on a road for a mile or mile and one-half to a large level clearing. At this point there is a beautiful view of Paulina Peak. The ski trail is marked slightly to the right across the flat. It then enters the trees again until it crosses road #2121.

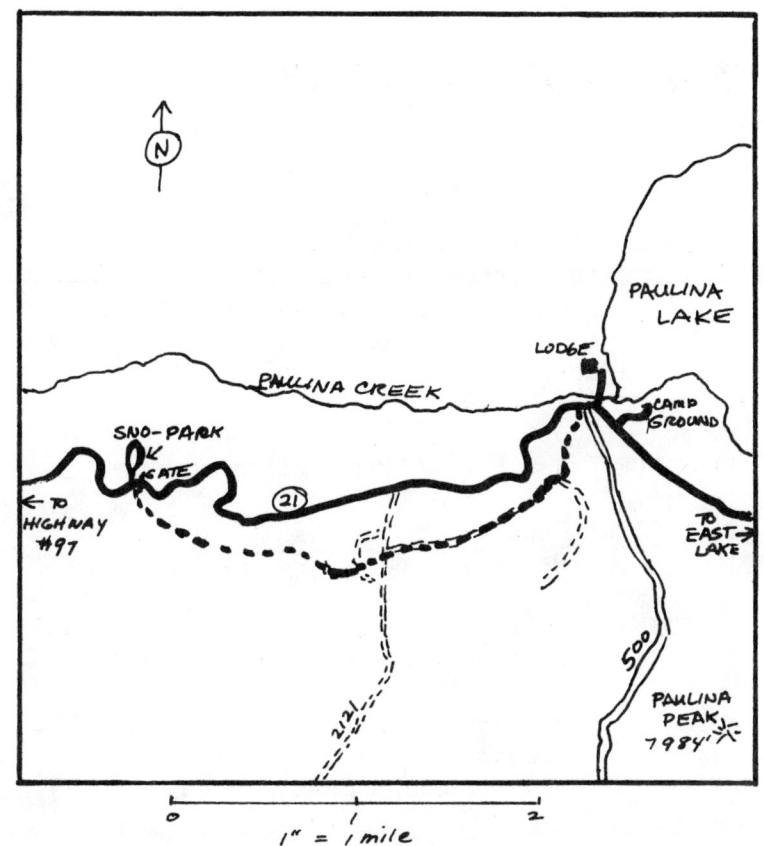

Follow the markers, on uphill, on roads and on a ski trail through the trees until it comes out on to the highway just before reaching Paulina Lake. The lodge and restaurant at Paulina Lake are open all winter. They have good, hot cinnamon rolls! There are also cabins to be rented in winter as well as summer.

59 PAULINA PEAK

STARTING POINT: Paulina Lake, just across from the road leading into Paulina Lake Lodge. Either ski up to here from the sno-park or make the trip late in the spring after the road to the lake has been plowed.

DISTANCE: About 4 1/2 to 5 miles one way

ELEVATION: Paulina Lake - 6,331'
Paulina Peak - 7,984'

TERRAIN: Uphill on a road, steady up the hill but not too steep

MAPS: USDA Forest Service: Deschutes National Forest
USGS: Paulina Peak, Oregon 7.5' 1963

Starting at the Paulina Lake junction of roads #21 and #500, go on road #500 to the south. This is the Paulina Peak road. It is a moderate, steady uphill all of the way. As the road circles around the south side of the peak, there are good views to the west and then to the south.

Near the top, the road winds through the trees and is more level until the last little uphill to the top. From the top, the view of the whole Newberry Crater is spectacular.

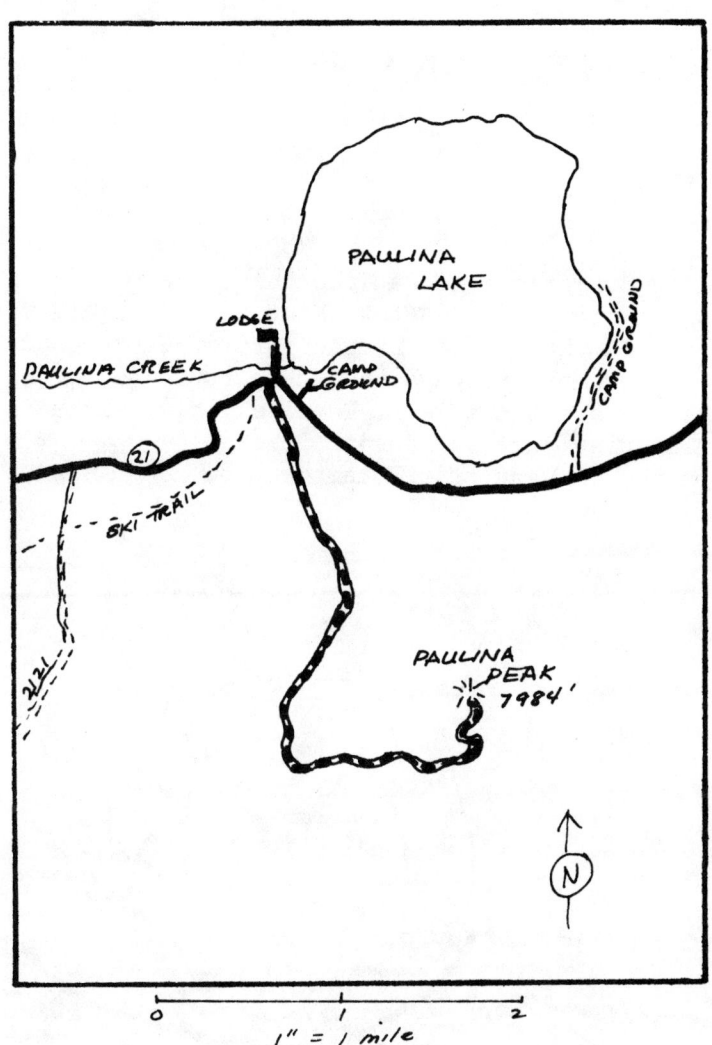

60 LITTLE CRATER C.G.

Follow directions to Paulina Lake. From there stay on road #21. After about two miles, there is a left turn into Little Crater Campground. The road goes through the campground along the lake for about a mile of level skiing. There is a nice view across Paulina Lake to Paulina Peak from the far end of the campground.

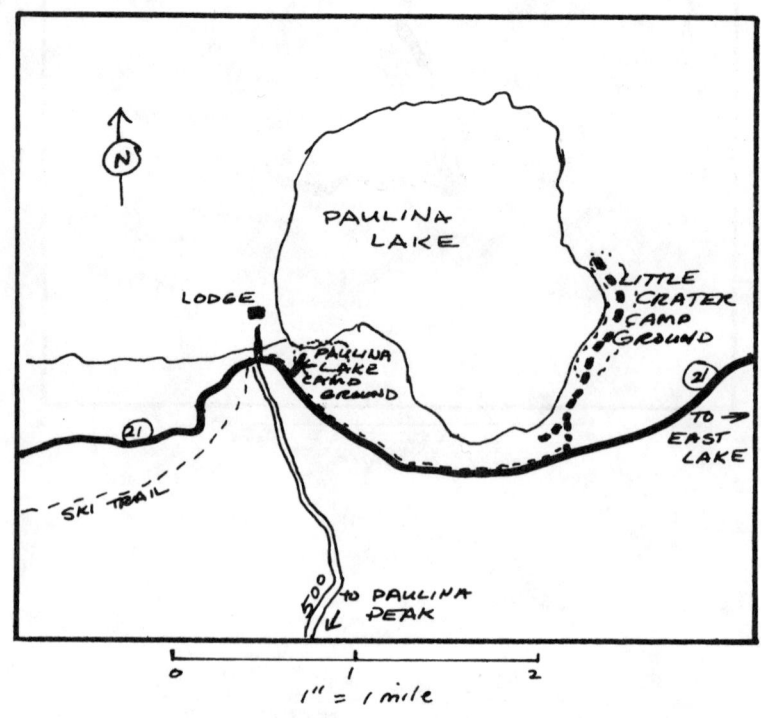

61 EAST LAKE

Follow directions to Paulina Lake. From there stay on the main road #21. It is about five miles to East Lake. On the right you will pass the obsidian flow. (This is a good destination for a shorter ski trip.)

At East Lake the area of the hot springs makes a good destination, or you can continue on around the lake to Cinder Hill Campground.

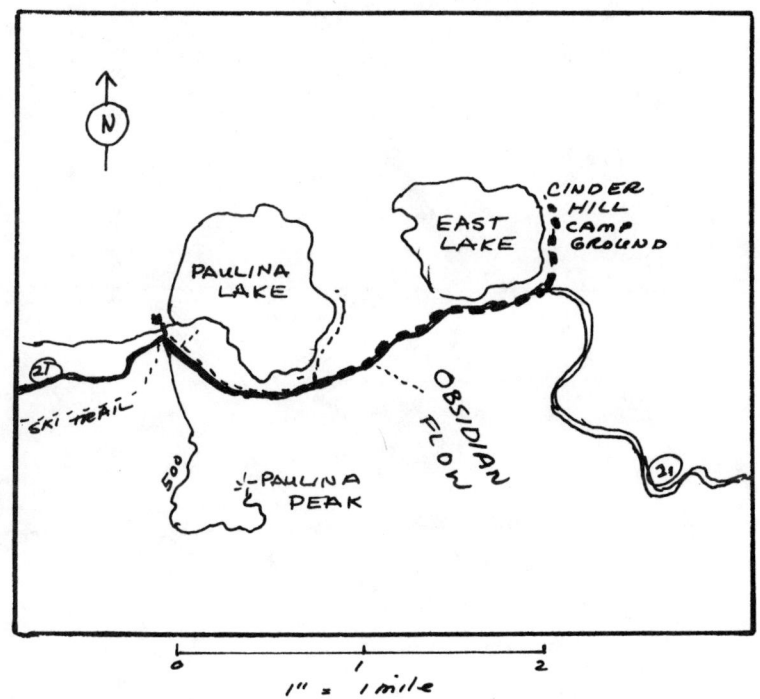

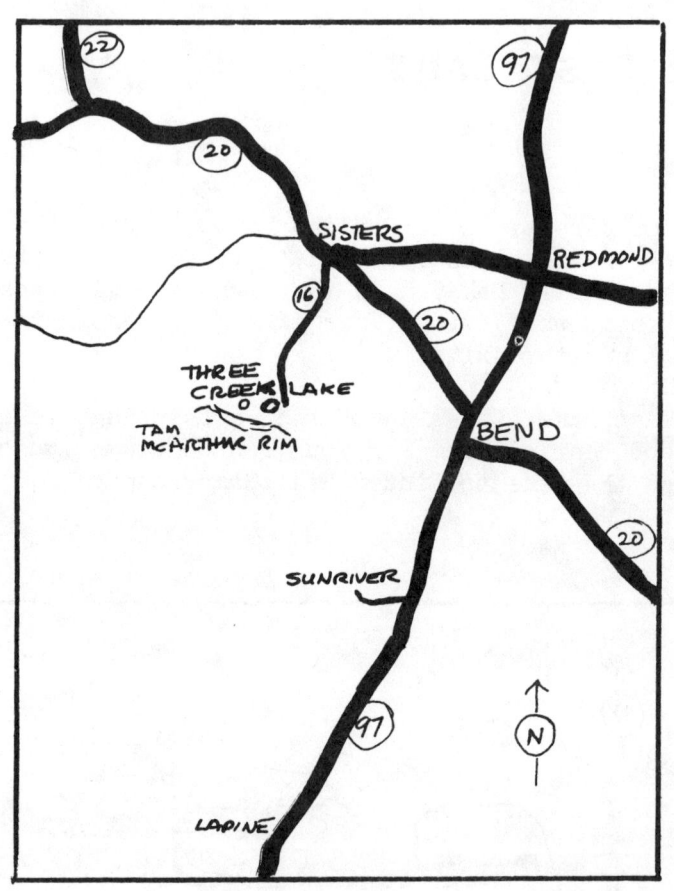

Tam McArthur Rim

SECTION 6

THREE CREEK LAKE

No.		Page
62.	Three Creek Lake	122
63.	Little Three Creek Lake	124
64.	Tam McArthur Rim	126

62 THREE CREEK LAKE

STARTING POINT: Turn south from Highway 20 on Elm Street in the middle of the town of Sisters. There is a sign pointing to Three Creek Lake (road #16). There is a new sno-park about eleven miles up the road at the snow gate, near road #1620. (An alternate sno-park is at Black Pine Spring which will be used if the road cannot be plowed to the upper lot.)

DISTANCE: About 6 1/2 miles one way

ELEVATION: Black Pine Spring - about 4,400'
Sno-park at road #1620 - about 5,000'
Three Creek Lake - about 6,500'

TERRAIN: Gentle to moderate hills. Trail is narrow in places and would be difficult with icy snow conditions

MAPS: USDA Forest Service: Deschutes National Forest
USGS: Broken Top, Oregon, 15' 1959

The marked ski trail starts to the right just past the snow gate. It follows an old road uphill through the trees most of the way. Now and then there are open slopes. By watching closely, a view of the Three Sisters can be seen to the west about half way up the trail. After about 4 miles, the ski trail comes out on to road #16. From there continue right on the main road (also used by snowmobilers). It is about 2 1/2 miles to the lake.

Three Creek Lake is at the bottom of Tam McArthur Rim. There is an excellent view of the whole rim. Return trip can be either back down the ski trail or down the main road.

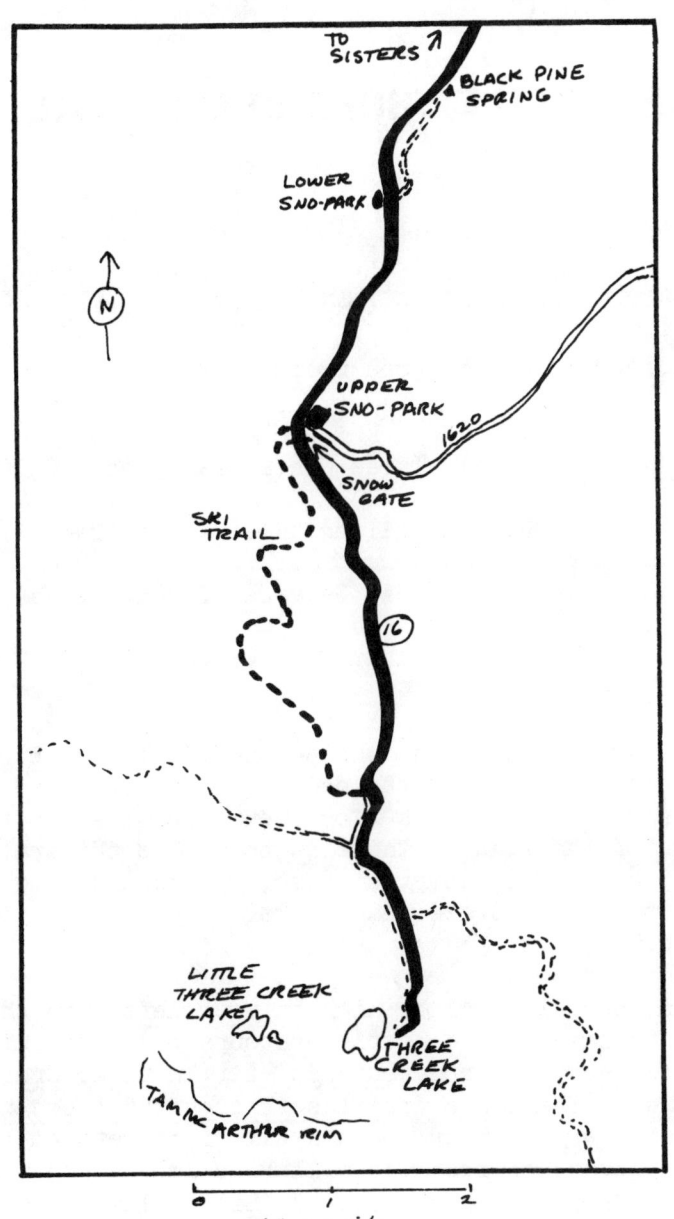

63 LITTLE THREE CREEK LAKE

STARTING POINT: Either ski to Three Creek Lake or in the late spring after the road is open, drive to Three Creek Lake.

DISTANCE: About three miles round trip

ELEVATION: Three Creek Lake - about 6,500'
Little Three Creek Lake- Abt. 6,700'

TERRAIN: Gentle rolling hills, open trees

MAPS: USDA Forest Service: Deschutes National Forest
USGS: Broken Top, Oregon, 15' 1959

At Three Creek Lake ski to the right, counterclockwise, across the dam. Follow the road along the campgrounds for about 1/2 mile to the end of the road. There is no marked ski trail, but by heading straight west, you should come to Little Three Creek Lake. Refer to your contour map.

McArthur Rim will be high on your left, so that by following the gentle contours below the rim, it is easy to come out at Little Three Creek Lake. There are openings through the trees all of the way. There is a small ridge between the two lakes, so that you will be climbing and then will drop slightly down to Little Three Creek Lakes. (There is a small lake first, then the main, larger lake.)

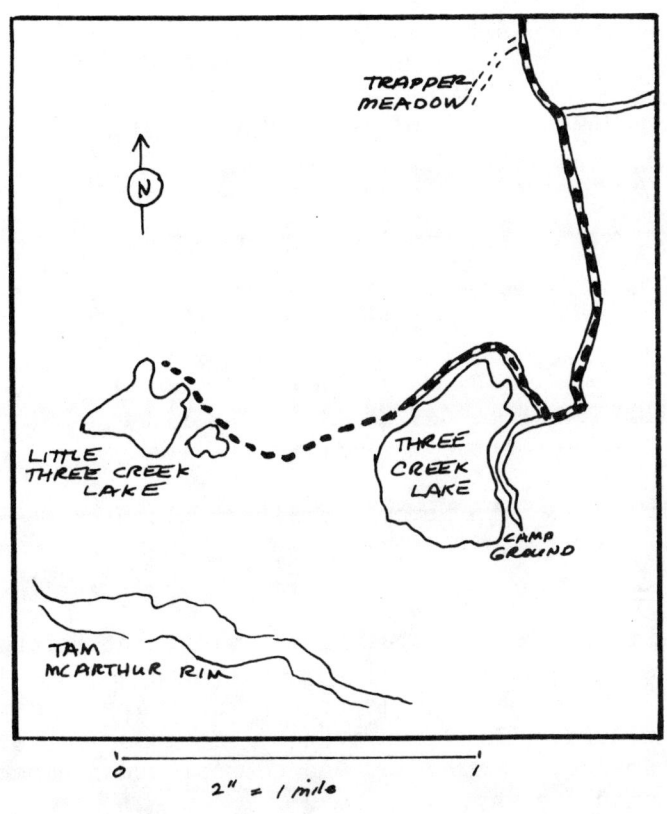

64 TAM MC ARTHUR RIM

STARTING POINT: Either at Three Creek Lake or at the junction of roads #16 and #370.

DISTANCE: Up the ridge - about 3 miles from Three Creek Lake
Around road #370 - about 7 miles one way from the junction

ELEVATION: Three Creek Lake - about 6,500'
Tam McArthur Rim - highest point 7,732'

TERRAIN: More difficult up the ridge
Gentle terrain on the road

MAPS: USDA Forest Service: Deschutes National Forest
USGS: Broken Top, Oregon 15', 1959

McArthur Rim is a beautiful viewpoint high above Three Creek Lake. The advanced skier will find this a worthwhile trip. There are no marked trails. This is a trip for someone who feels comfortable using map and compass and landmarks to find the way.

There are two approaches to the rim:

1. This tour is about three miles from Three Creek Lake one way. Starting at Three Creek. Lake follow the ridge to the left. This starts to the left just before the concession building, leading up through the trees on to the east end of Tam McArthur Rim. Angle right on to the rim. Once on the rim the trees become more open so that you can see where you are going. Watch for cornices along the edge of the rim. Sometimes these are quite large and can break off with the weight of the skier.

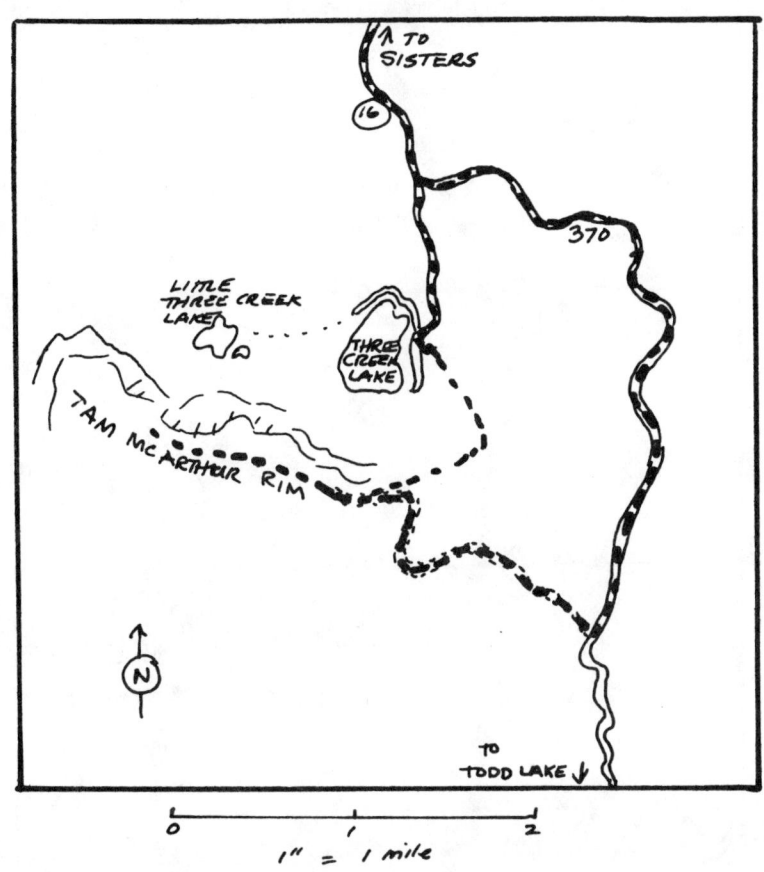

2. A longer but easier way to approach the rim is to follow road #370. (About 7 miles from the junction of roads #16 and #370.) This is the road which goes south to Todd Lake. To approach the rim follow the road about 4 or 4 1/2 miles. Then go right to the west through the woods uphill on to the rim. If there is deep snow it may be difficult to see where the road is. If this happens you will have to follow the contours on the map (or, the snowmobiles may already have a trail following the road).

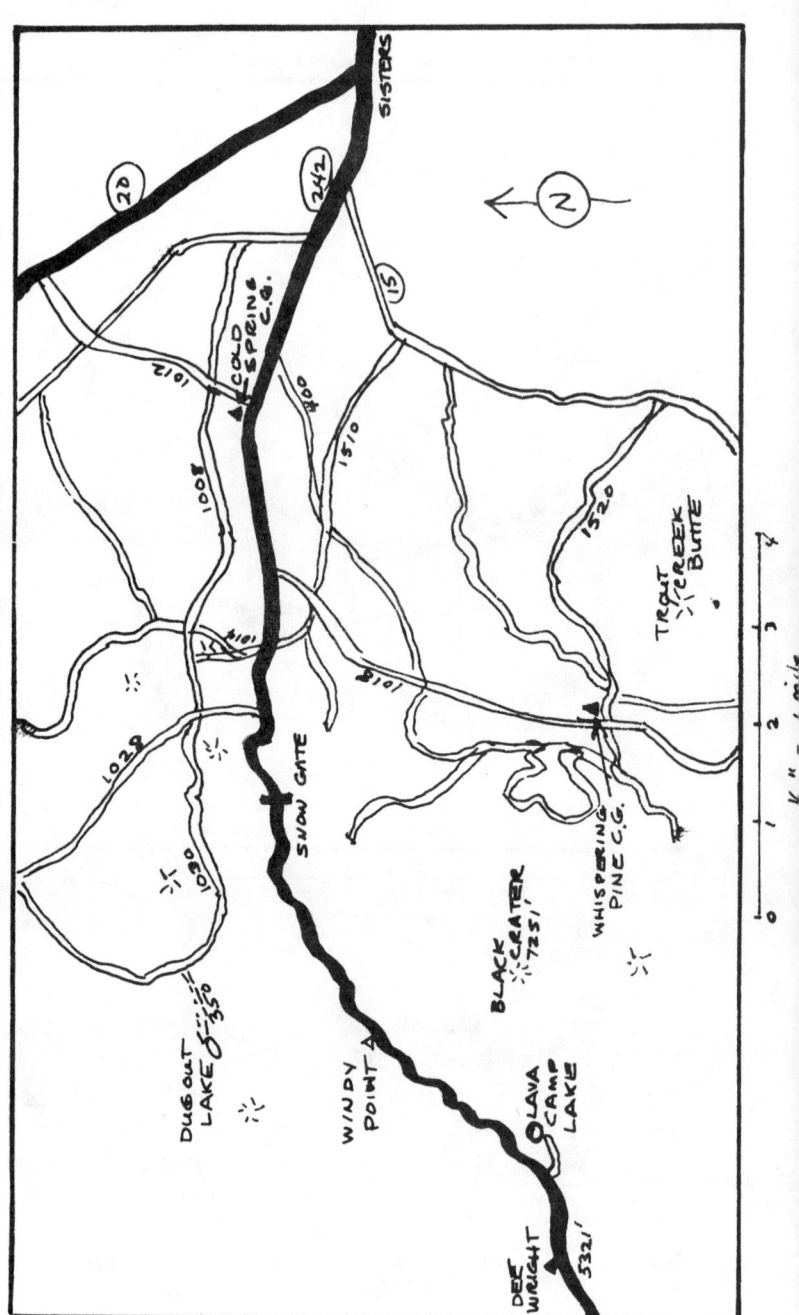

SECTION 7

McKENZIE

No.		Page
65.	McKenzie - Lower Elevation Roads . . .	130
66.	Dugout Lake.	132
67.	McKenzie Pass.	134
68.	Windy Point.	136
69.	Dee Wright Observatory	136
70.	Lava Camp Lake	137

65 MC KENZIE
lower elevation roads

STARTING POINT: Drive west from Sisters on the McKenzie Pass Highway #242. Go as far as it is plowed, or it there is enough snow, ski on any of the side roads wherever you can park.

DISTNACE: Follow back roads as far as you like.

ELEVATION: Town of Sisters: 3,184'
7 miles west of Sisters: 4,100'

TERRAIN: Gentle roads, easy skiing

MAPS: USDA Forest Service: Deschutes National Forest
USGS: Sisters, Oregon 15' 1959

There are quite a number of side roads, forest roads, which go off the McKenzie Highway. If there is enough snow, any of them are good skiing. Some of them are:

1. Road #1012 near Cold Springs Campground. Ski about 1/2 mile north to a junction with road #1008. To the left is a good road which leads to the vicinity of Fourmile Butte and Graham Butte.

2. Road #1014 near Fourmile Butte. Ski north to where there is a choice of roads leading to Fourmile Butte, Graham Butte and Sixmile Butte.

3. Road #1018. This road travels south into the vicinity of Whispering Pine Campground and Trout Creek Butte.

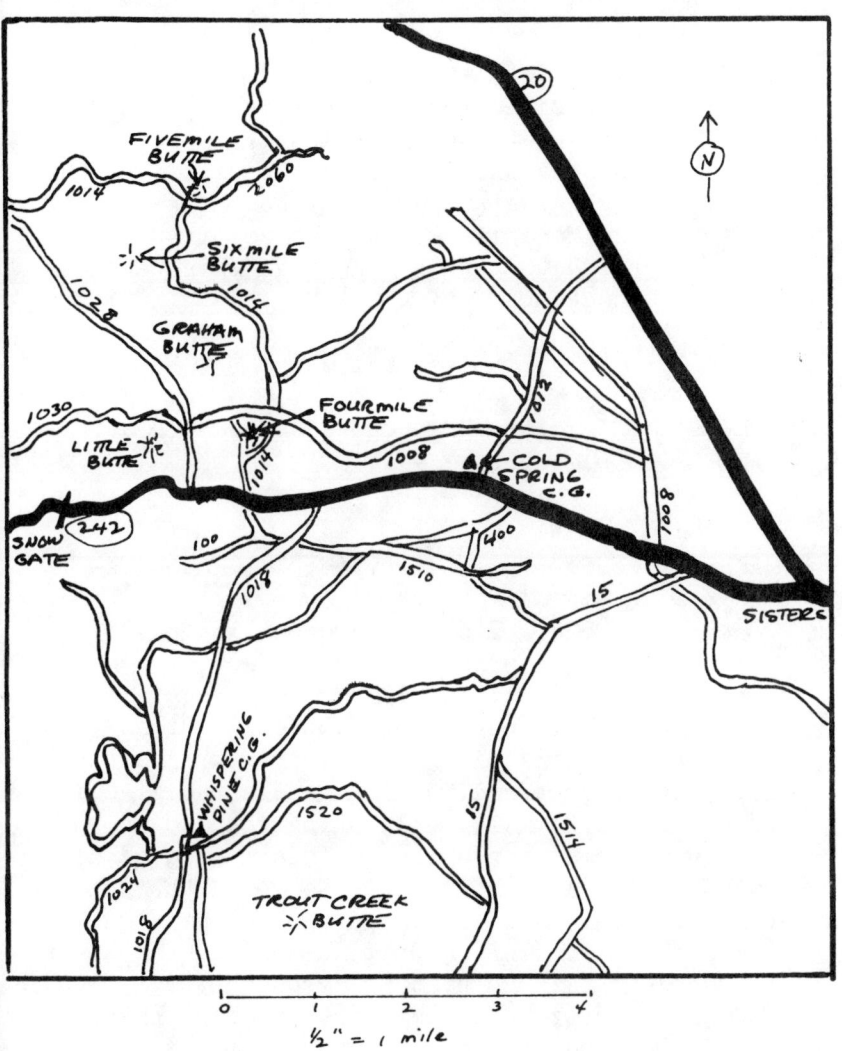

66 DUGOUT LAKE

STARTING POINT: Drive west from Sisters on the McKenzie Highway #242. Seven and one half miles from Sisters is a "four corners" at the junction of road #1028. This is the last cross roads before the highway starts steeply up the curves of the McKenzie Pass. There is usually room to turn around and park at this junction.

DISTANCE: About 6 miles one way

ELEVATION: Junction of road #1028 - 3,800'
Dugout Lake - 4,900'

TERRAIN: Gentle roads

MAPS: USDA Forest Service: Deschutes National Forest
USGS: Sisters, Oregon 15', 1959
Three Fingered Jack, Oregon 15', 1959

From the four corners on the McKenzie Highway go north about one mile to a four-way junction. Turn left on road #1030. A gentle uphill climb of about 1 1/4 miles will bring you to an open area with some open hills. This is a good destination for a short trip. To go on to Dugout Lake, the main road is ahead and to the right across the open flat. Continue Following road #1030 on uphill and past Bluegrass Butte. Road #350 turns west to Dugout Lake up where the road levels out and begins to start down a little. (There should be a sign, but I think this one is often gone.)

The road goes west for about one mile to Dugout Lake. Past Dugout Lake the ridge to the right and to the west offers a spectacular view of Mt. Washington. It is well worth the little extra climb to get the view. There are also excellent open slopes up there for telemark turns.

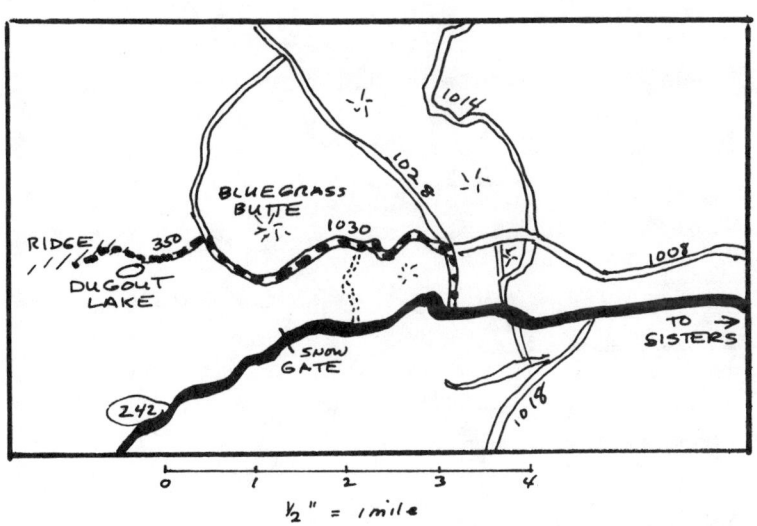

Spring skiing at Dugout Lake

67 MC KENZIE PASS

STARTING POINT: Drive west from Sisters on Highway #242 toward the McKenzie Pass. It is 8 1/2 miles to the snow gate. If the road is not plowed to the snow gate, park at the junction of road #1028 which is just at the bottom of the hill where the road starts up the curves of the McKenzie. If you park here, it is about one mile to the snow gate.

DISTANCE: From the snow gate one way to:
Windy Point - 3.2 miles
Dee Wright - 6.7 miles
Lava Camp Lake - abt. 6 1/2 miles

ELEVATION: Snow gate - 3,900'
Windy Point - 4,909'
Dee Wright - 5,309'
Lava Camp Lake - 5,280'

TERRAIN: Moderate uphill on a road

MAPS: USDA Forest Service: Deschutes National Forest
USGS: Sisters, Oregon 15', 1959
Three Fingered Jack, Oregon 15' 1959

The views from the top of the McKenzie Pass are exceptional. From the Dee Wright Observatory the peaks of the Oregon Cascades to the north and south are visible. Belknap Crater and the whole expanse of the lava beds are just in front of you to the north. To the south are the lava beds leading to the North Sister and Black Crater.

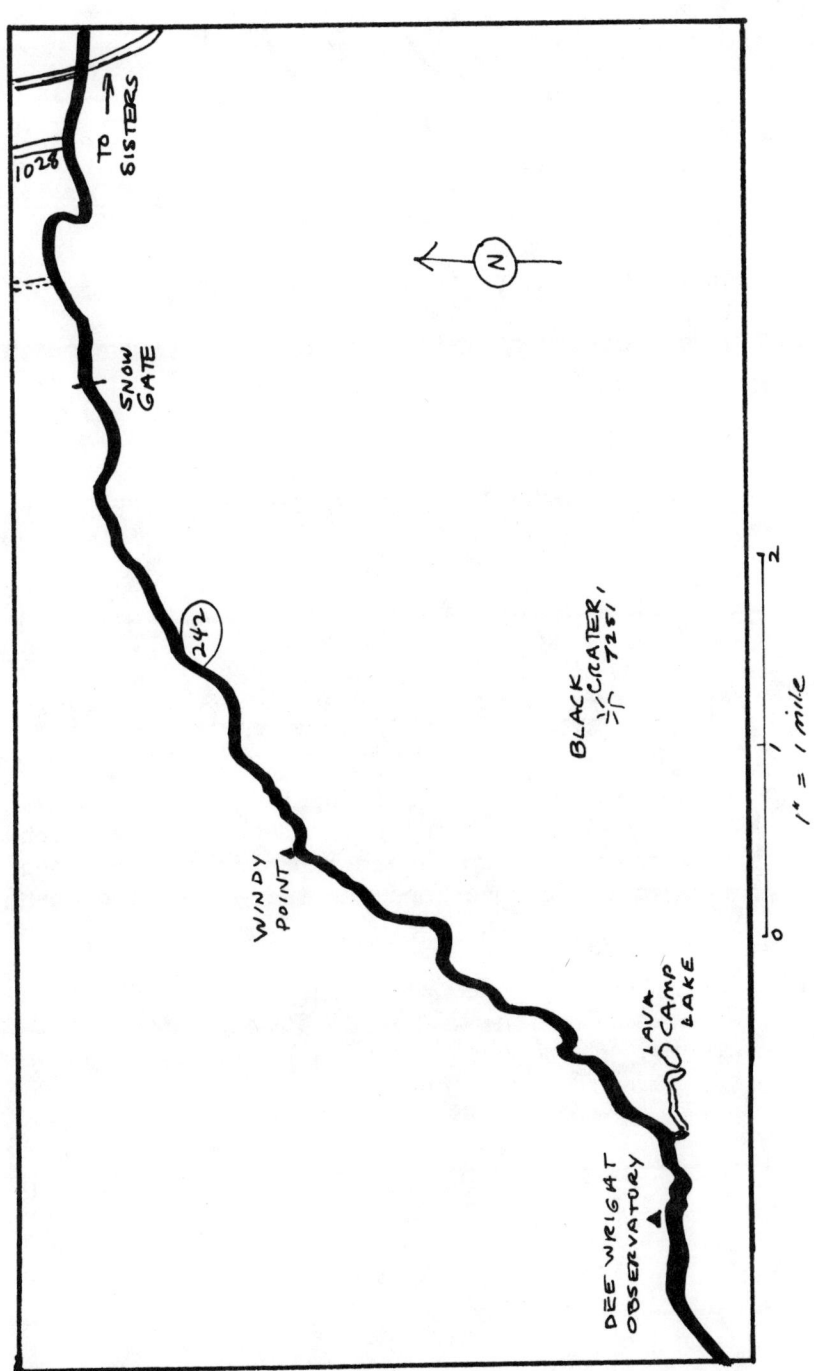

68 WINDY POINT

From the snow gate, ski up the main highway. It is moderate uphill all of the way (which is a nice downhill run coming back).

Windy Point is well named. It is an open, rocky outcropping near the edge of the lava beds. Often the wind will have blown all the snow away so that the pavement is bare here.

There is a good view of Mt. Washington, Belknap Crater and the lava beds.

69 DEE WRIGHT OBSERVATORY

From the snow gate, ski up the main highway. Continue on past Windy Point. The road, which has been mostly uphill to Windy Point, becomes more gentle beyond here and there are more open views of the lava beds.

Near the top of the pass, the road goes between some interesting and very photogenic lava formations. There are some wind-blown old snags in this area too. Cornices and snow drifts are often very unusual.

Dee Wright Observatory is located on the open flat at the summit of the pass. On a stormy day it can be very windy and cold. Visibility may be very poor. Go prepared, as the weather can change rapidly.

70 LAVA CAMP LAKE

Follow the main road above the snow gate for six miles. The road into Lava Camp Lake is to the left just as the highway enters the rugged lava formations. It is about 1/2 mile from the highway back into the lake. Around on the south side of the lake is an open front shelter.

The Pacific Crest Trailhead is just before you get to the lake and on the right.

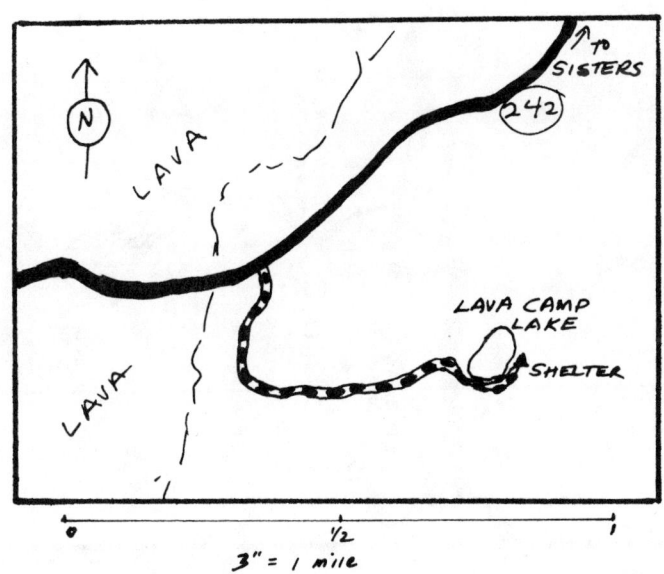

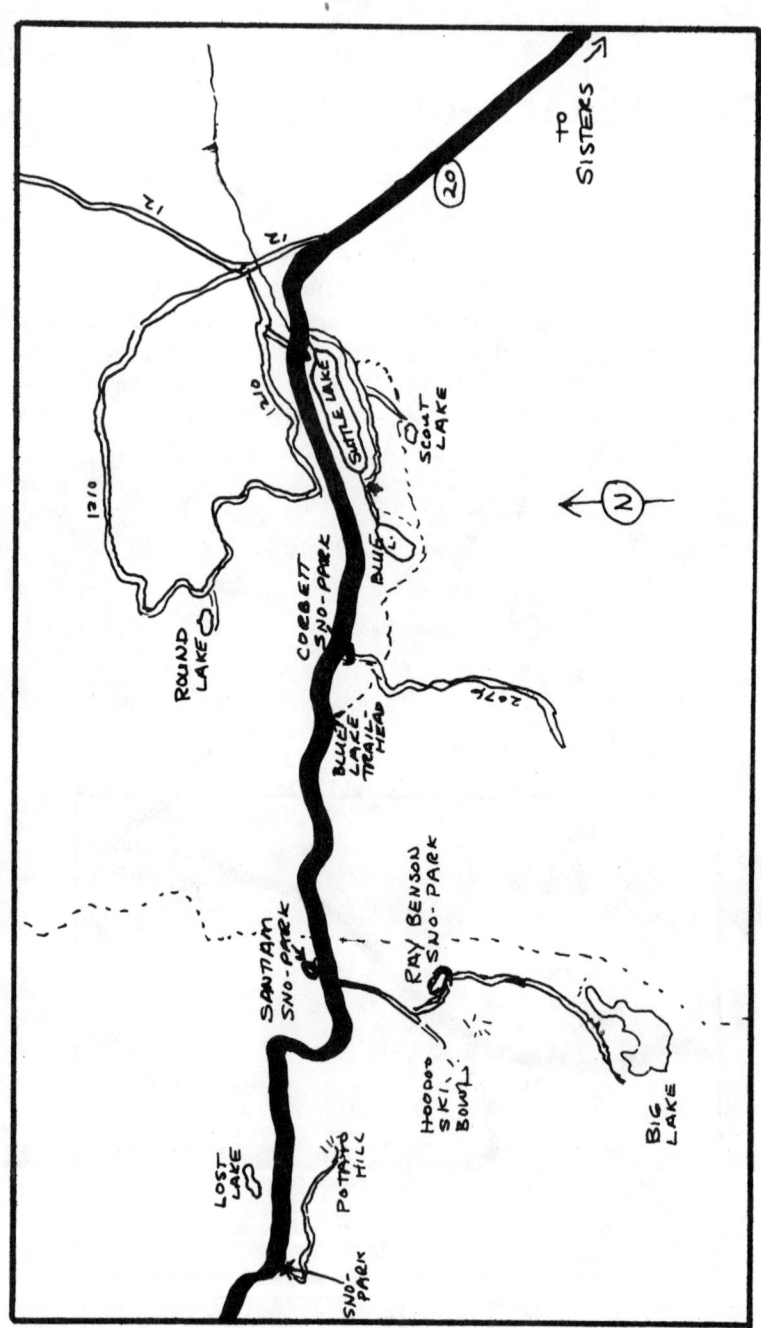

SECTION 8

SANTIAM PASS

No.		Page
71.	Suttle Lake.	140
72.	Scout Lake Loops	142
73.	Corbett State Park	144
74.	Round Lake	146
75.	Corbett Sno-park	148
76.	Blue Lake Trail	149
77.	Ray Benson Sno-park	150
78.	North Loop Trail	152
79.	South Loop Trail	153
80.	Big Lake	154
81.	Little Nash	156
82.	Potato Hill	158
83.	Big Meadows	160
84.	Fay Lake	160

71 SUTTLE LAKE

STARTING POINT: Thirteen miles from Sisters on highway #20. Drive around Suttle Lake to plowed parking at the west end by the Alpine Restaurant.

DISTANCE: About 4 miles around the lake

ELEVATION: 3,438 at Suttle Lake

TERRAIN: Mostly flat, through trees

MAPS: USDA Forest Service: Deschutes National Forest
USGS: Sisters, Oregon 15', 1959
Three Fingered Jack, Ore. 15' 1959

Suttle Lake Trail is a marked loop trail around the lake. It can be started anywhere around the lake. Since plowed parking is available near the Alpine Restaurant that seems to be a good starting point.

The trail is close enough that the lake is visible most of the time. At the lower end of the lake, where Lake Creek runs out, the ski trail goes down stream to cross a footbridge. At the east end of the lake, in the campground, there is an open front shelter.

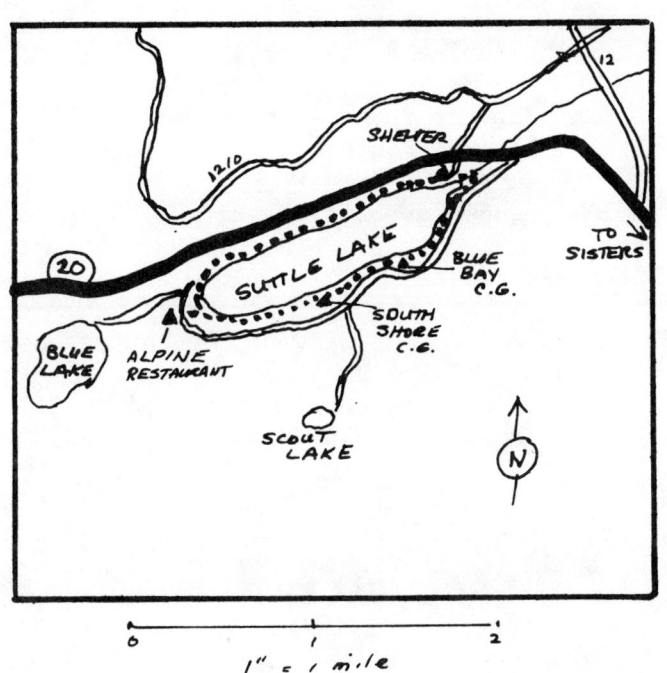

72 SCOUT LAKE LOOPS

STARTING POINT: Thirteen miles from Sisters on highway #20. Drive around Suttle Lake to plowed parking at the west end near the Alpine Restaurant.

DISTANCE: Shorter route - about 3 miles
Longer route - about 4 miles

ELEVATION: 3,439' at Suttle Lake

TERRAIN: Moderate

MAPS: USDA Forest Service: Deschutes National Forest
USGS: Sisters, Oregon 15', 1959
Three Fingered Jack, Ore. 15' 1959

Starting from the Alpine Restaurant, cross the road to Link Creek Campground. Follow the marked ski trail to the right around the lake.

At Blue Bay Campground, there is a trail junction. One trail continues around the lake. The trail to the right starts uphill and crosses the road. Across the plowed road, the trail enters the trees, going gently uphill on a forest road which comes out near Scout Lake. There is a new shelter this year at Scout Lake. From Scout Lake there are two routes:

1. Shorter route: Follow the main road from Scout Lake back down to South Shore Campground. From there return to the lake trail and go left back to the parking lot.

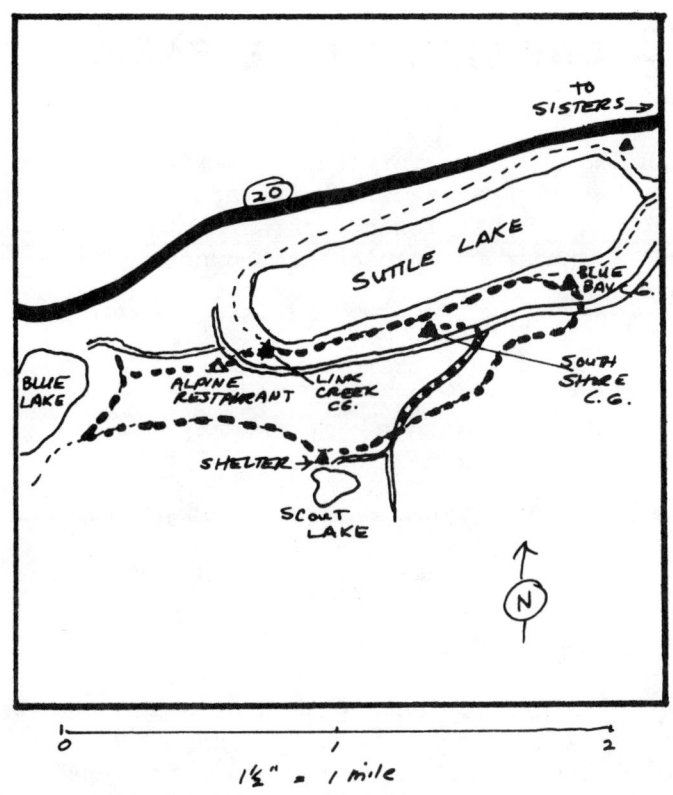

2. Longer route: At Scout Lake continue to the right on around the lake. Follow the trail markers uphill. The trail then starts down a long hill toward Corbett State Park. At the bottom of the hill and through the woods is a junction. Turn right to return to Blue Lake and back to Suttle Lake.

73 CORBETT STATE PARK

STARTING POINT: Thirteen miles from Sisters on highway #20. Drive around Suttle Lake to the plowed parking at the west end near the Alpine Restaurant.

DISTANCE: About 3 miles round trip

ELEVATION: Suttle Lake - 3,438'

TERRAIN: Quite easy

MAPS: USDA Forest Service: Deschutes National Forest
USGS: Sisters, Oregon 15', 1959
Three Fingered Jack, Ore. 15' 1959

From parking at the Alpine Restaurant ski west on the marked trail toward Blue Lake. At the end of the open flat the trail turns uphill to the left. It then climbs gently to the junction of the trail which comes from Scout Lake. Go to the right on varied terrain. It is about 3/4 mile on to Corbett State Park.

There is another trail to Corbett State Park which starts high up on highway #20 and comes downhill to the park. This is the Blue Lake Trail. This is a good loop trail with a car at each end.

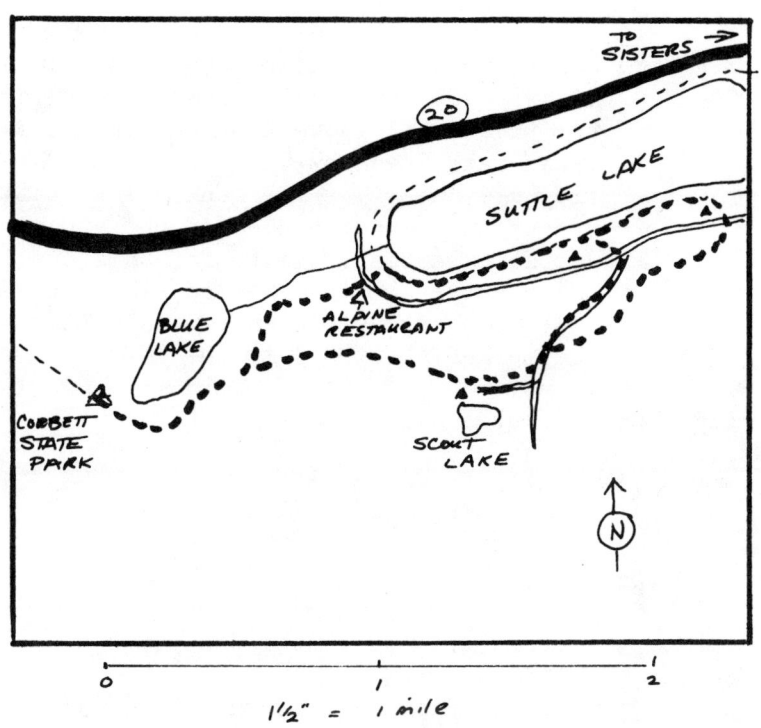

74 ROUND LAKE

STARTING POINT: Thirteen miles from Sisters on highway #20 at Suttle Lake. Parking for this trail is west of the bridge across Lake Creek by the road into Suttle Lake Resort. The marked ski trail starts on the north side of the highway. Another starting point for this trail is to drive north on road #12 about a mile to the junction where #1210 starts the marked ski trail to the left.

DISTANCE: About 5 miles one way

ELEVATION: Suttle Lake - 3,438'
Round Lake - 4,280'

TERRAIN: Moderate uphill

MAPS: USDA Forest Service: Deschutes National Forest
USGS: Sisters, Oregon 15', 1959
Three Fingered Jack, Ore. 15' 1959

The marked ski trail starts on the north side of the highway (or at the road #1210 trailhead). After a short distance through the trees, the trail turns left on to road #1210. From here it follows this road all the way to Round Lake. This road goes through the woods and along logged areas. There are some good view points.

There is also a shorter loop which turns off of road #1210 after about 2 miles. There is a marked trail to the right and slightly downhill. This comes back into #1210 almost at the junction with #12. This is a 4 mile loop.

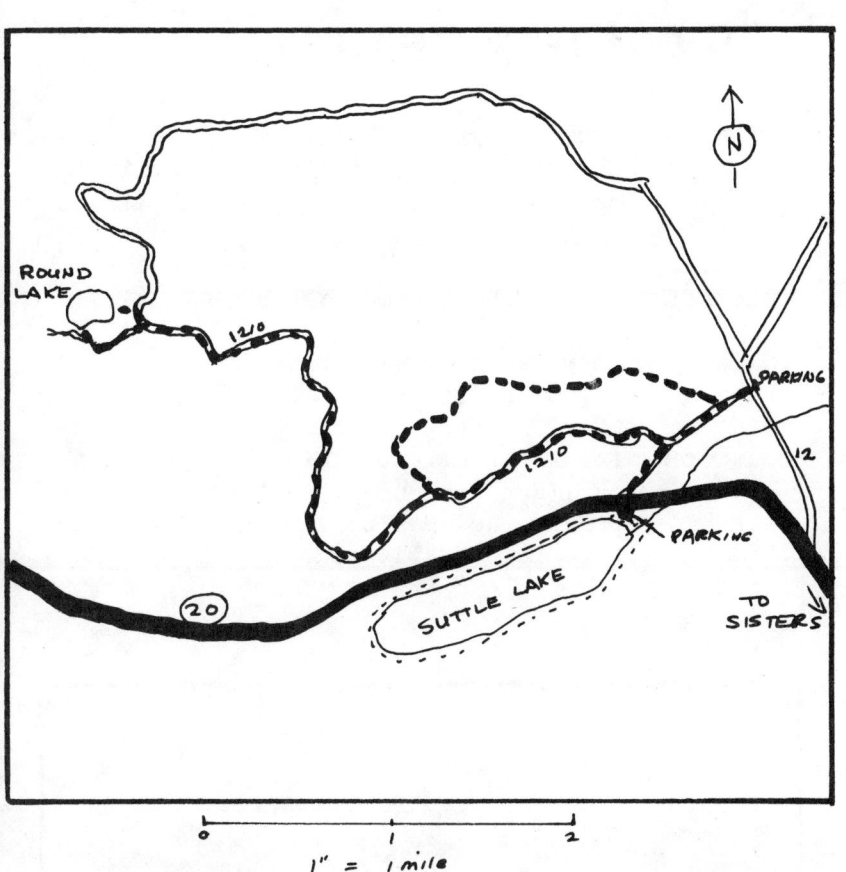

75 CORBETT SNO-PARK

STARTING POINT: Sixteen or seventeen miles from Sisters on highway #20 near the Suttle Lake grade. This is a new sno-park being built in 1984.

ELEVATION: At Corbett Sno-park about 4,482'

This is a new area of development. Watch for maps of new trails in this area. Contact the Sisters Ranger District of the Deschutes National Forest for information. This sno-park is the end of the 7 1/2 miles which starts at Ray Benson Sno-park and includes part of the North Loop Trail, Circle Lake Trail and the Island Lake Trail.

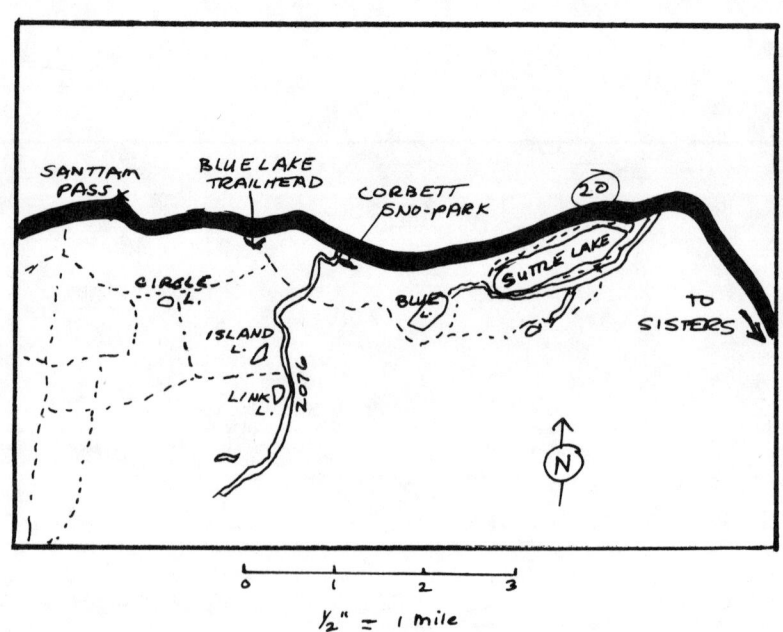

76 BLUE LAKE TRAIL

The Blue Lake Trail is a marked ski trail starting at a small turn out sno-park about one mile west of the Corbett Sno-park. There is a Blue Lake Trailhead sign where the trail starts. It is a rather steep downhill trail all the way to Corbett State Park. Beyond Corbett Park the trail becomes variable on out to Blue Lake and Suttle Lake. Leave a car at each end to make this a loop trail. Trail is about 3 1/2 miles.

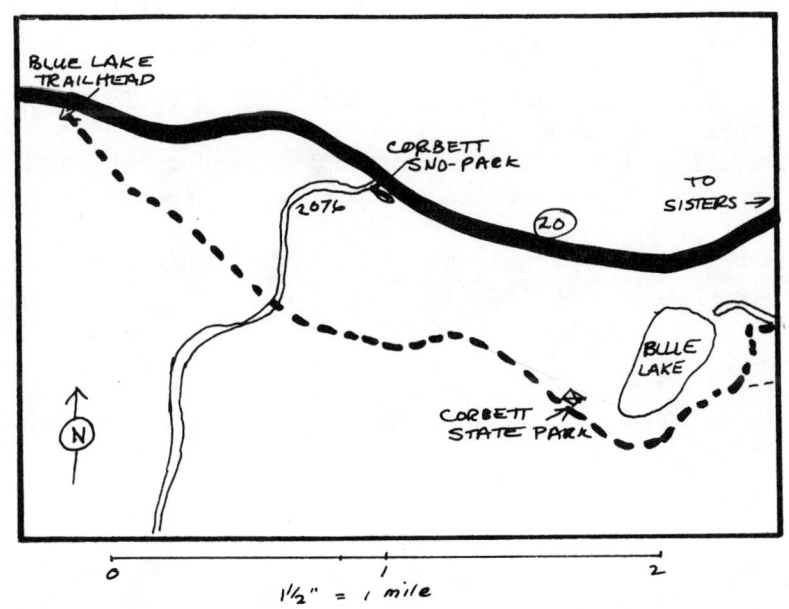

77 RAY BENSON SNO-PARK

STARTING POINT: Ray Benson Sno-park is near Hoodoo Ski Bowl. Turn off highway #20 at the sign. Drive about one mile and just before the road starts down into Hoodoo turn left on the road to Ray Benson Sno-park.

ELEVATION: 4,800'

TERRAIN: Easy to moderate on most trails

MAPS: USDA Forest Service: Willamette National Forest
USGS: Three Fingered Jack, Ore. 15' 1959

From Ray Benson Sno-park there is a variety of marked ski trails to choose from. Most are loop trails. Snowmobiles are not allowed on the ski trails. The trail which goes to Corbett Sno-park also starts here. There are two new, longer loop ski trails being developed which should be open and marked within another year.

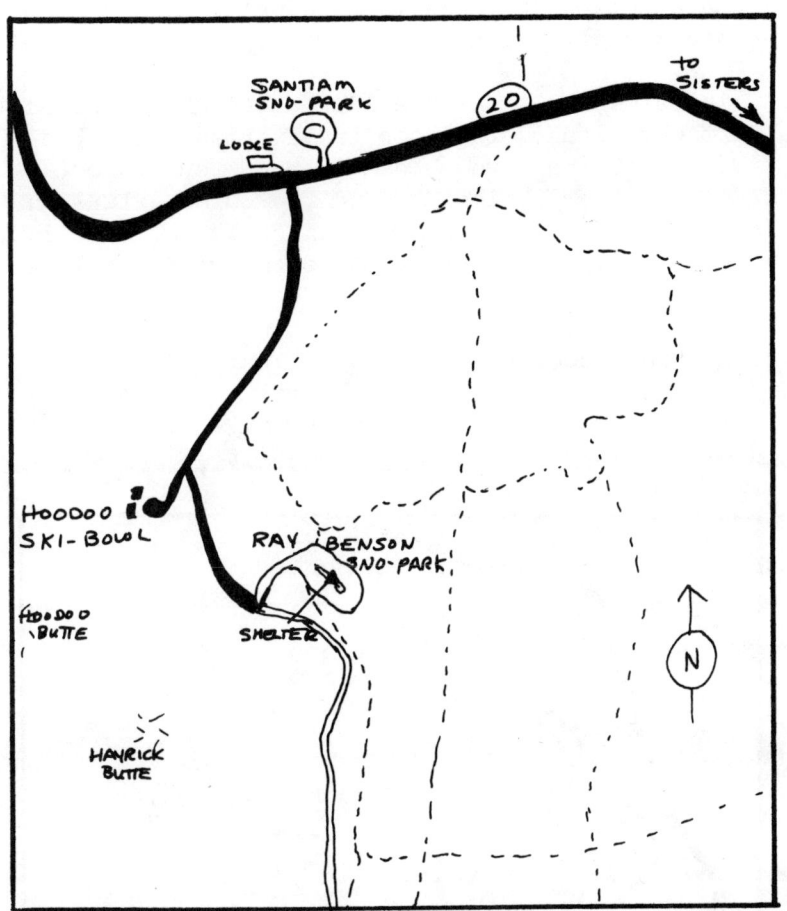

78 NORTH LOOP

The North Loop Trail begins at the northwest corner of the parking lot. After the trail crosses an open area and enters the woods there is a junction which is the beginning of the loop. Preferred direction is clockwise.

This is mainly a ski trail cut through the woods. Part way around, the loop trail crosses the Pacific Crest Trail which can be used for a shorter loop. After skiing around the outer extension of the loop it will again cross the Pacific Crest Trail as it continues back to the parking lot.

Check snow conditions before starting out too far on this trail. It is mainly in the trees and can have a lot of icy tree-wells. There is a new shelter scheduled to be built part way around the loop (see map).

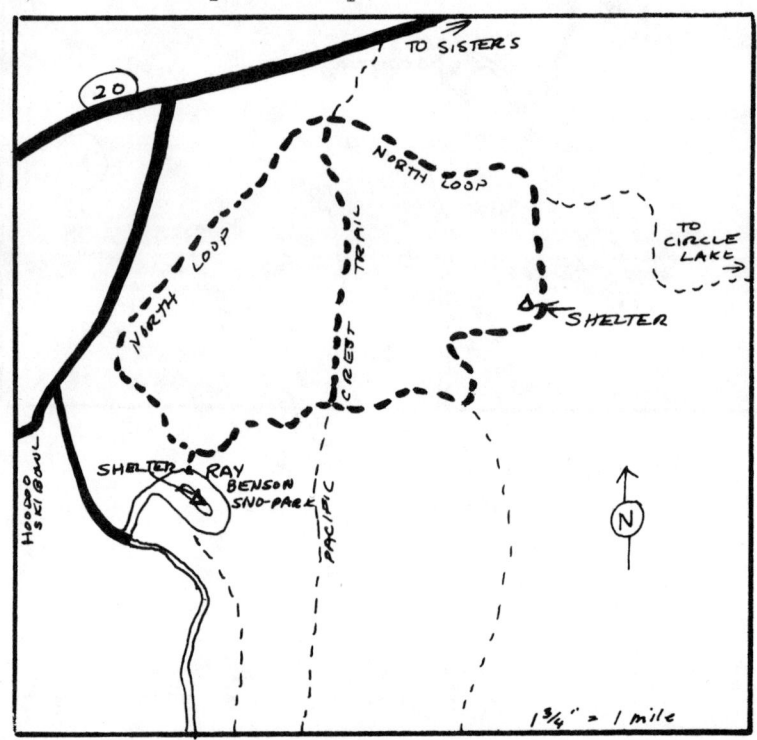

79 SOUTH LOOP

This marked ski trail starts from the south side of the Ray Benson Sno-park. First you cross an open flat, then across the snowmobile trail. From there the marked trail runs parallel to the Big Lake road (which is a groomed snowmobile trail). There is a short loop and a longer loop. To make the shorter loop take the south cut-off. Part of the return loop of this trail is the Pacific Crest Trail and then on the North Loop Trail. The far end of the longer loop is almost to Big Lake. To ski clockwise around, start on the north loop.

These are open easy trails through the Airstrip Burn of August, 1967.

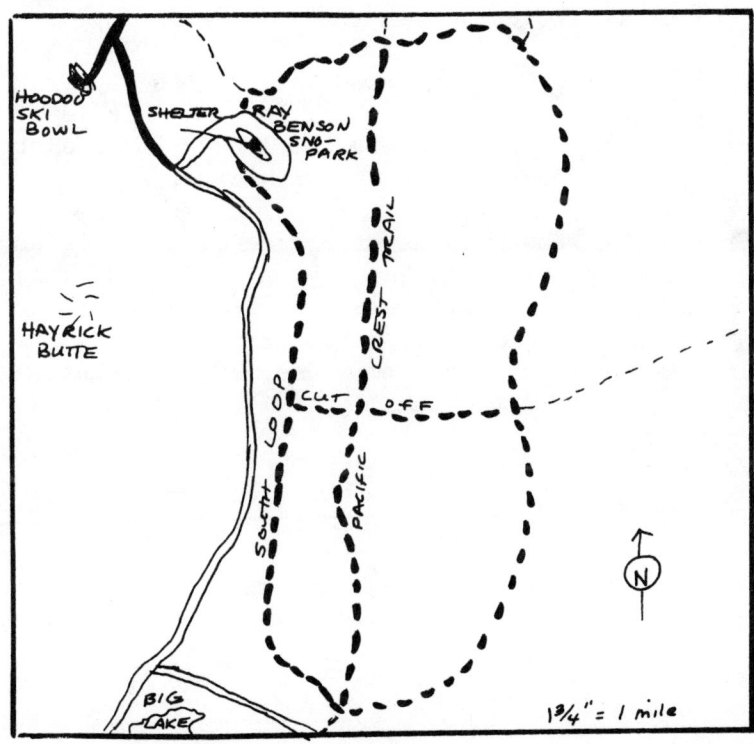

80 BIG LAKE

There are two alternatives for skiing to Big Lake:

1. Follow the South Loop Trail to where it turns back north. From there go cross country to the right (west) over to the lake.

2. Follow the Big Lake road all of the way from Ray Benson Sno-park to Big Lake. This is a very easy way to ski to the lake. It is also a snowmobile road so ski with care.

From the northwest side of Big Lake, there is an excellent view of Mt. Washington. As you make the ski trip into Big Lake, Mt. Washington is in front of you going in. Three Fingered Jack is in front as you come out. Use extreme caution about skiing on the lake.

Along the South Loop trail to Big Lake

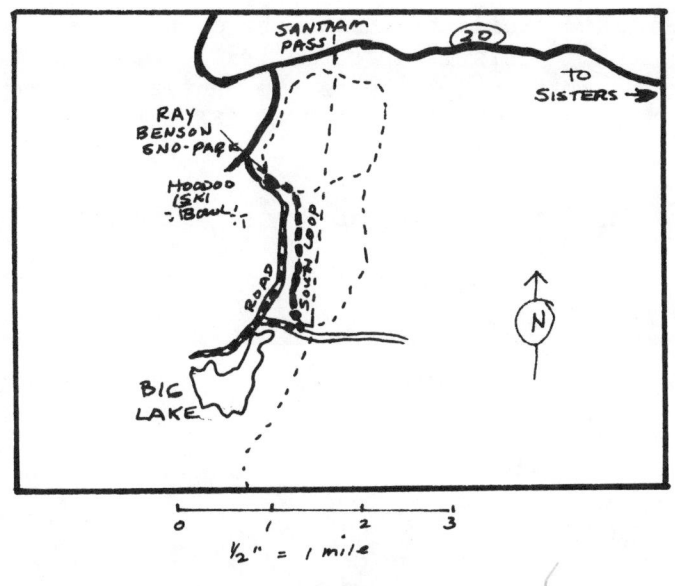

81 LITTLE NASH

STARTING POINT: Little Nash Sno-park is about one mile west of Santiam Junction on highway #20.

DISTANCE: One mile of trail. Open flat beyond there for practice.

ELEVATION: About 3,700'

TERRAIN: Flat, very easy

MAPS: USDA Forest Service: Willamette National Forest
USGS: Three Fingered Jack, Ore. 15' 1959

The marked trail begins at the east end of the sno-park. This is a gentle trail along an old logging road which leads to Santiam Airstrip. The open flat at the end of the trail makes a good practice area.

Road #1370 to Little Nash Crater also begins at this sno-park.

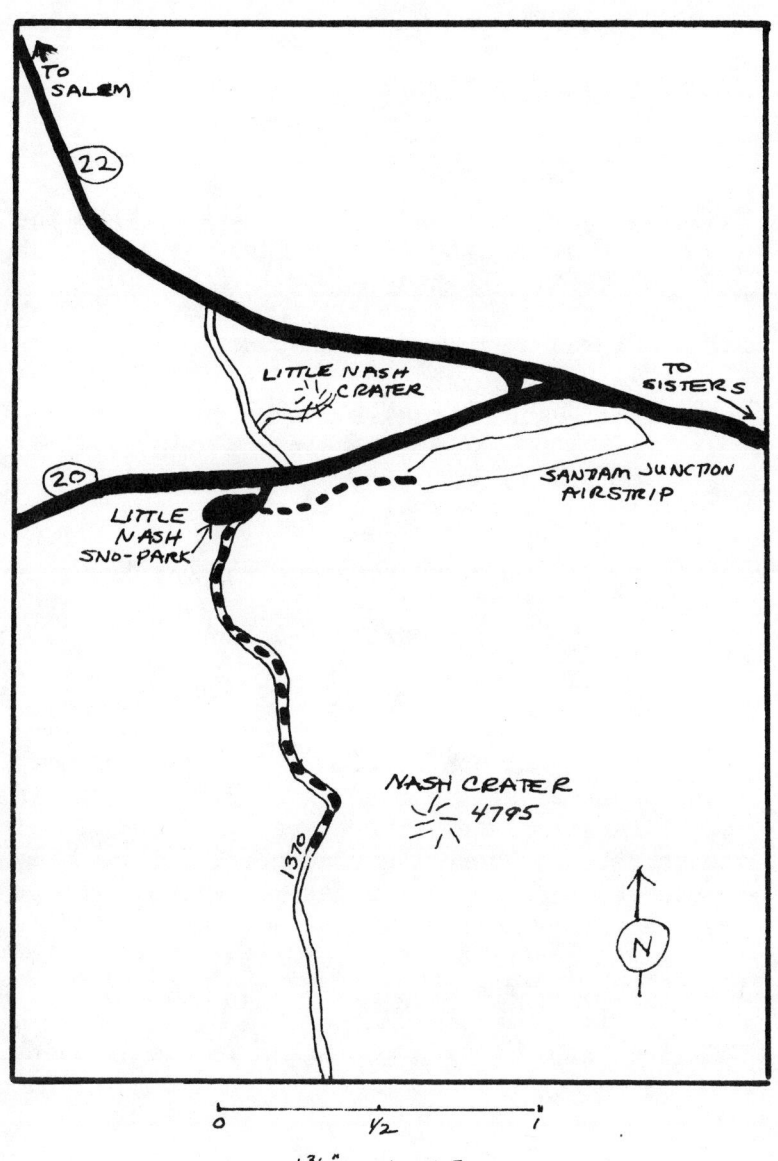

82 POTATO HILL

STARTING POINT: Potato Hill Sno-park is at the top of the long highway hill by Lost Lake. (Highway #20)

DISTANCE: About two miles one way

ELEVATION: Sno-park - about 4,083'
End of road on hill - about 5,000'

TERRAIN: Moderate uphill all the way

MAPS: USDA Forest Service: Willamette National Forest
USGS: Three Fingered Jack, Ore. 15' 1959

This trail is an uphill road all of the way. It is not marked but the road is easy to follow. In two different places, there are open slopes. If you cannot see where the road goes, ski part way across the open until you can see where the road again enters the trees. The end of the road is on the ridge near the top of Potato Hill. The top is in the trees.

This trip has lots of open hills for telemarking.

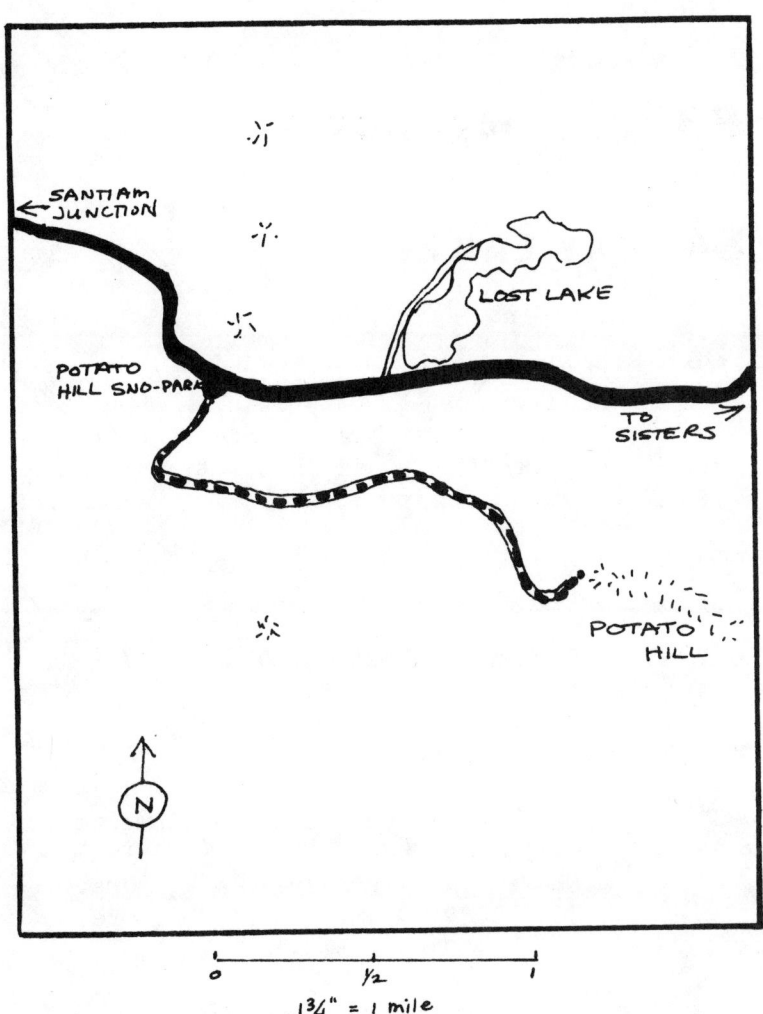

83 BIG MEADOWS

84 FAY LAKE

STARTING POINT: Park by the highway at the Big Meadows road #2267. This is about 5 or 6 miles north of Santiam Junction on highway #126. It is about ten miles south of Marion Forks.

DISTANCE: Big Meadows - 1 3/4 miles one way
Fay Lake - 3 miles one way

ELEVATION: Parking - about 3,400'
Fay Lake - 3,800'

TERRAIN: Moderate uphill

MAPS: USDA Forest Service: Willamette National Forest
USGS: Three Fingered Jack, Ore. 15' 1959 - Mt. Jefferson, Ore. 15' 1959

This ski trail is all on roads. The first mile is gradually uphill on road #2267. Then go left on road #2257. This is gradually downhill through the woods as far as Big Meadows. The restrooms at Big Meadows will probably be open. Shortly beyond Big Meadows, the road crosses the North Santiam River. From here continue following road #2257 on uphill to Fay Lake.

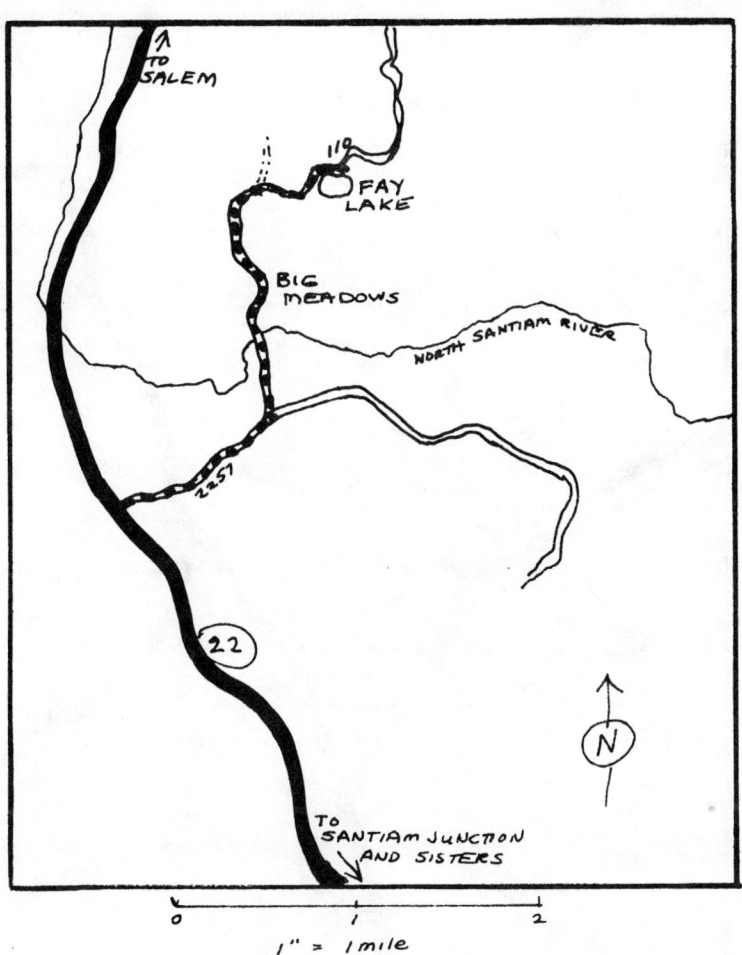

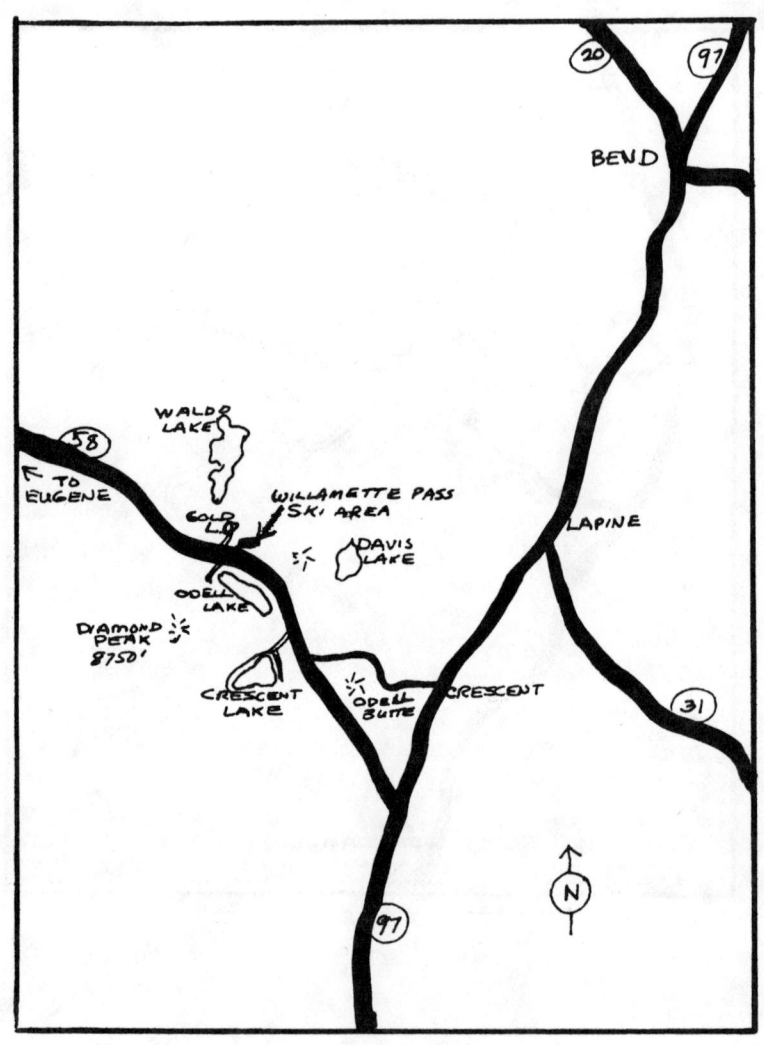

SECTION 9

WILLAMETTE PASS

No.		Page
85.	Rosary Lakes.	164
86.	Pacific Crest Trail Loop.	166
87.	Gold Lake	168
88.	Marilyn Lake.	169
89.	Pengra Pass Trails.	170
90.	Maklaks	172
91.	Fawn Lake from Crescent Lake.	174
92.	Fawn Lake from Odell Lake	175
93.	Odell Meadows	176
94.	Odell Butte	177

85 ROSARY LAKES

STARTING POINT: Willamette Pass Sno-Park at the summit of highway #58.

DISTANCE: About 3 miles one way

ELEVATION: Lower Rosary Lake - 5,707'
Willamette Summit - 5,126'

TERRAIN: Moderate uphill

MAPS: USGA Forest Service: Willamette National Forest or Deschutes National Forest
USGS: Odell Lake, Ore. 7.5' 1963
Waldo Lake, Ore. 15' 1956

The marked trail goes northeast from Willamette Pass, past the highway department gravel storage shed, to where it joins the Pacific Crest Trail. It then follows the Crest Trail uphill through the woods along the side of the ridge. Near the top of the ridge, the trail becomes more gentle, with varied terrain, until it goes slightly down to Lower Rosary Lake.

If desired, the marked ski trail continues to the other two Rosary Lakes. There is a view of Rosary Rock from the lakes.

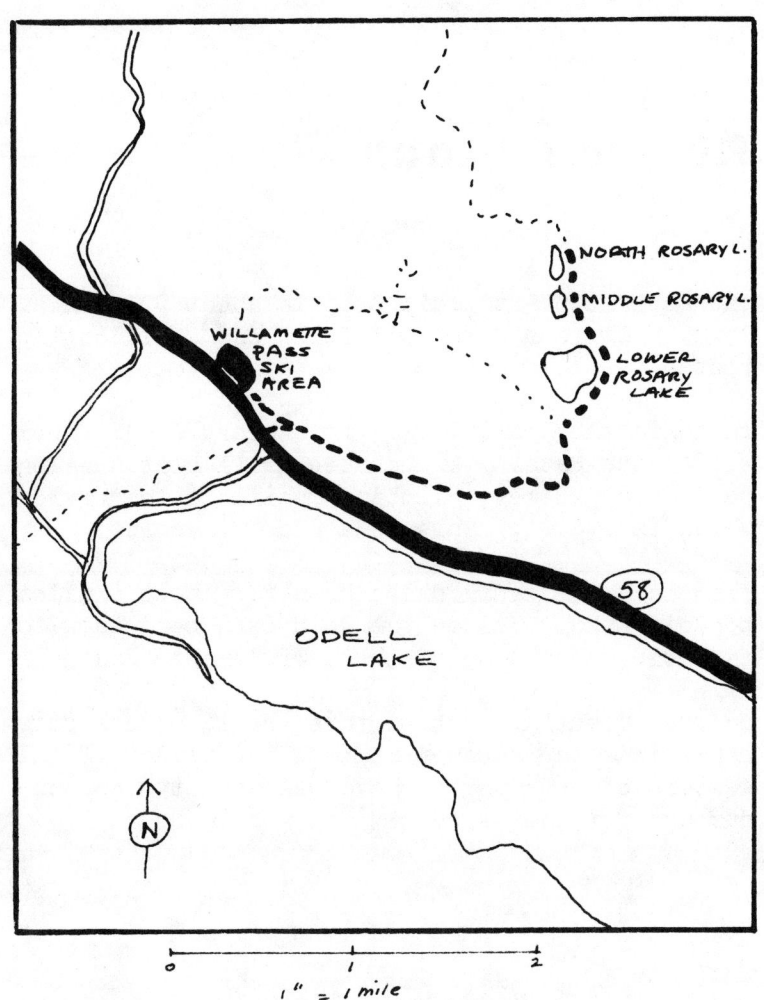

86 P.C.T. LOOP

The Pacific Crest Trail Loop is about 9 1/2 mis. long. It is a more difficult and challenging route.

To begin the trail, ski to Rosary Lakes from Willamette Pass. The marked trail continues on past Rosary Lakes, climbing uphill to the divide which is 6,200'. This is a nice viewpoint.

From here the trail drops down for about 4 miles to Gold Lake. Follow the Gold Lake road back to the Gold Lake Sno-park or to Willamette Pass.

Before starting out on this trail, check snow conditions and weather reports. Consider if all members of your party have the ability and endurance for the tour.

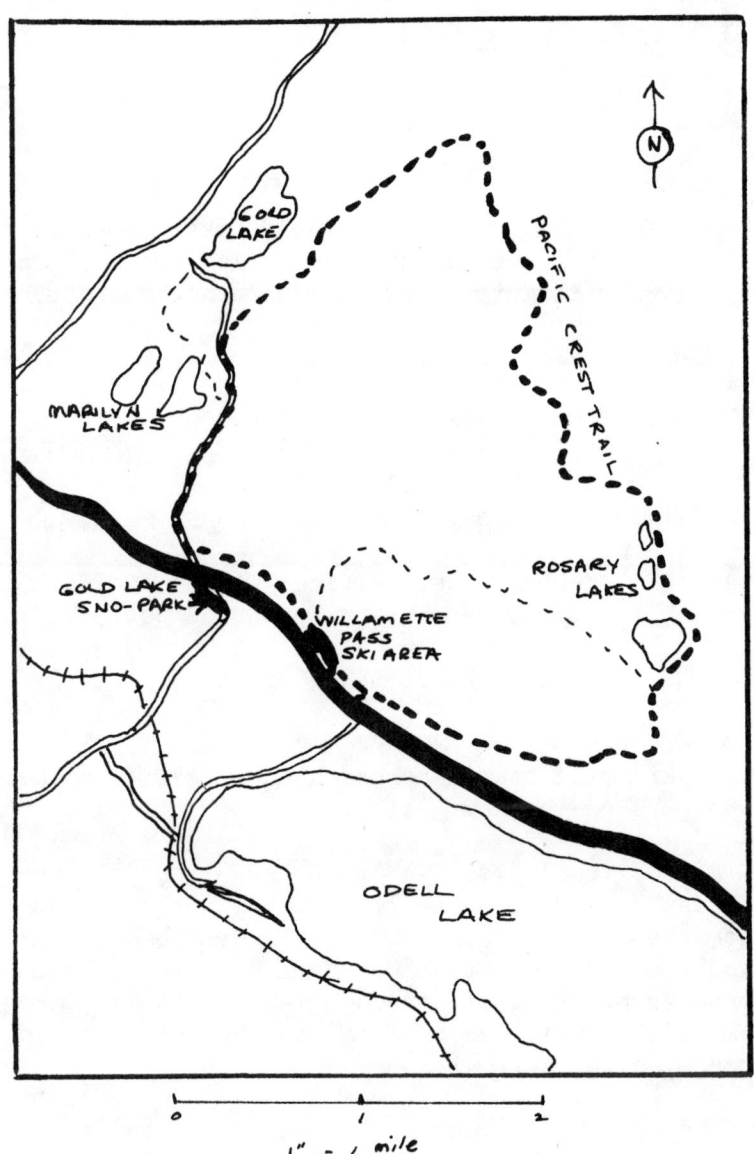

87 GOLD LAKE

STARTING POINT: Park at Gold Lake Sno-park. This is about one mile west of the Willamette Pass summit on highway #58.

DISTANCE: About 2 miles one way

ELEVATION: Gold Lake Sno-park - 5,000'
Gold Lake - 4,800'

TERRAIN: Very easy road

MAPS: USDA Forest Service: Willamette National Forest or Deschutes National Forest
USGS: Waldo Lake, Oregon 15' 1956

The ski trail starts across highway #58 from the sno-park on the north side.

A marked trail follows road #223 through the forest. The road is almost level, then drops somewhat downhill as you come to Gold Lake. As you come to the outlet of the lake, there is an open front shelter on the right. It is on a small hill with the back of the building to the road, so watch for it.

For a view of Diamond Peak, ski on to the north end of the lake on the Gold Lake Trail. Use caution about skiing on the lake. The ice may not be solidly frozen.

88 MARILYN LAKES

Ski on the Gold Lake Road #223 for about one mi. Watch for the Marilyn Lake Trail which goes down to the left from the road.

Thr trail drops down to Upper Marilyn Lake. From here it continues on to Gold Lake.

There is a short side trail which goes to Lower Marilyn Lake. From the lakes there is a view of Diamond Peak.

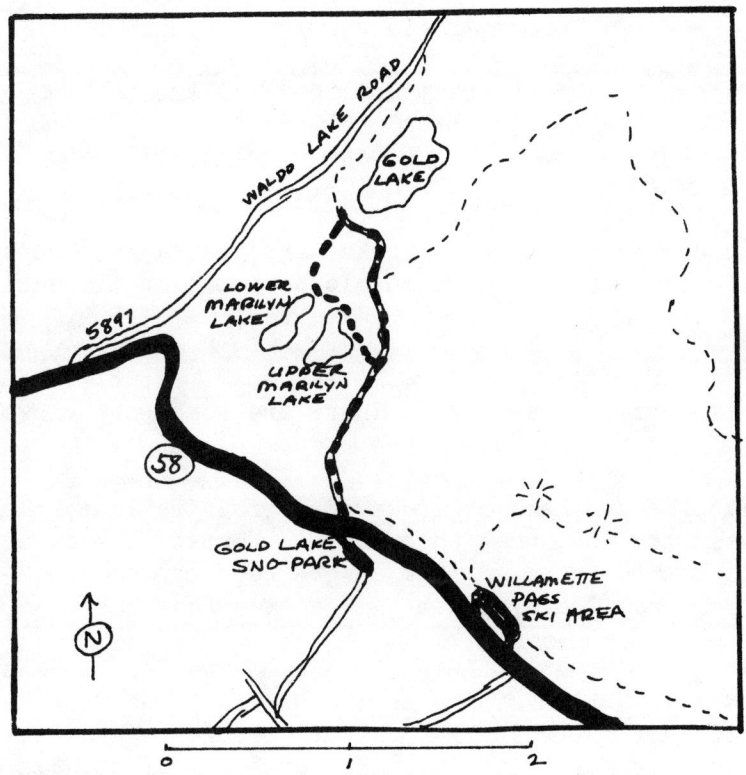

89 PENGRA PASS TRAILS

STARTING POINT: Gold Lake Sno-park, about one mile west of the summit to Willamette Pass on highway #58.

DISTANCE: Pengra Pass: about 1 1/2 miles one way
Other loop trips: 2 to 4 miles
Midnight Lake: about 3 miles one way

ELEVATION: Gold Lake Sno-park - 5,009'
Pengra Pass   - 5,003'
Midnight Lake   - about 5,360'

TERRAIN: Road from sno-park in - easy
Forest trails - more difficult

MAPS: USDA Forest Service: Willamette National Forest
USGS: Waldo Lake, Oregon 15' 1956

There are a number of marked ski trails and loops in this area. There should be a map at the sno-park.

For a very easy tour, ski the road about 1 1/2 miles to Pengra Pass. There are some open views out to the west along the road.

From Pengra Pass there are several trails to the west and southwest through the forest. Another loop trip is to go from Pengra Pass on the Pacific Crest Trail back to Willamette Pass.

To go to Midnight Lake go east on the Pengra Pass road a short distance to the Pacific Crest Trail. The Pacific Crest Trail south from here has ski trail markers almost to the north end of the lake where a short trail leads over to the lake.

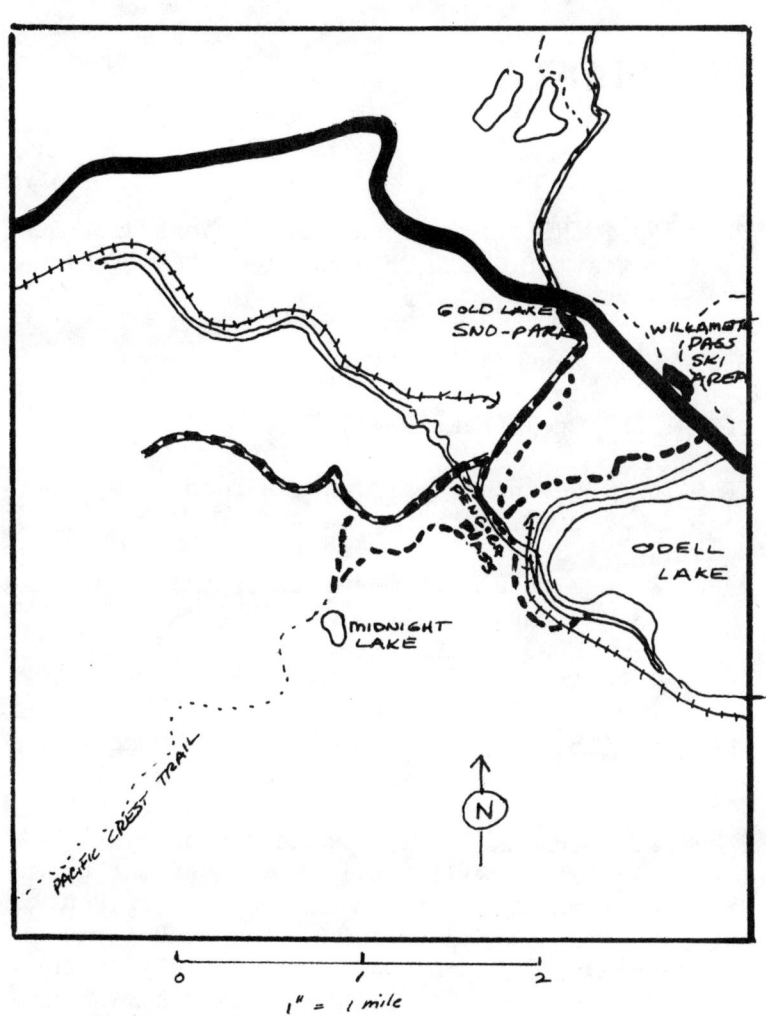

90 MAKLAKS

STARTING POINT: Limited parking a short distance west of Odell Creek to the side of highway #58.

DISTANCE: Seven mile loops

ELEVATION: Odell Lake - 4,787'

TERRAIN: Beginner trail on the road, more difficult loop in the woods

MAPS: USDA Forest Service: Deschutes National Forest
USGS: Odell Lake, Oregon 7.5' 1963

These trails begin down the old Davis Lake road, which is a short way west from the parking.

The road is blocked with rocks and dirt so that the ski trail will start down over the bank. The road through the trees is open and is gentle skiing. The marked trail off the road turns to the left making a loop which can be skied either way. The upper part of this trail follows Maklaks Creek part of the way.

There is a side trail which comes down to highway #58 at Sunset Cove and returns along the lake to the east end.

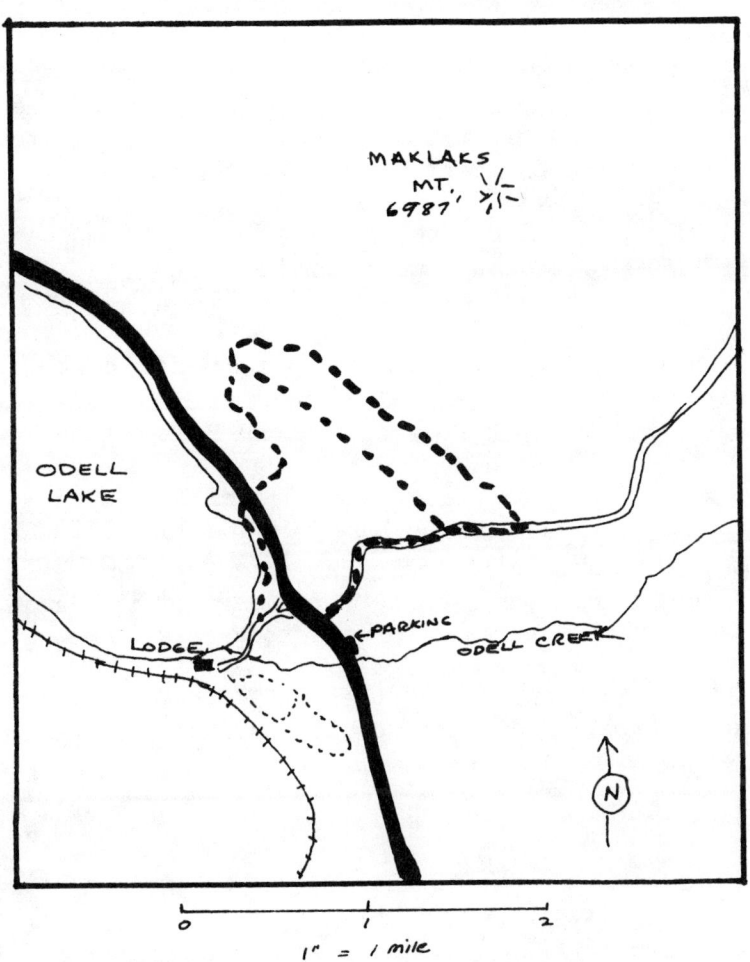

91 FAWN LAKE

from CRESCENT LAKE

STARTING POINT: From highway #58 turn south on the Crescent Lake road #60. Cross the railroad track and drive 1/4 mile to the Crescent Townsite Sno-park.

DISTANCE: 4 miles one way
ELEVATION: Crescent Lake Townsite - 4,475'
Fawn Lake - about 5,600'

TERRAIN: Uphill, moderate to more difficult
MAPS: USDA Forest Service: Deschutes National Forest, Diamond Peak Wilderness
USGS: Odell Lake, Oregon 7.5' 1963
Waldo Lake, Oregon 15' 1956

A marked ski trail begins at the Crescent Lake Townsite Sno-park. The first part of the trail is on varied terrain through lodgepole woods.

After about one mile, the trail traverses along a hillside and then continues into more open woods on up to Fawn Lake.

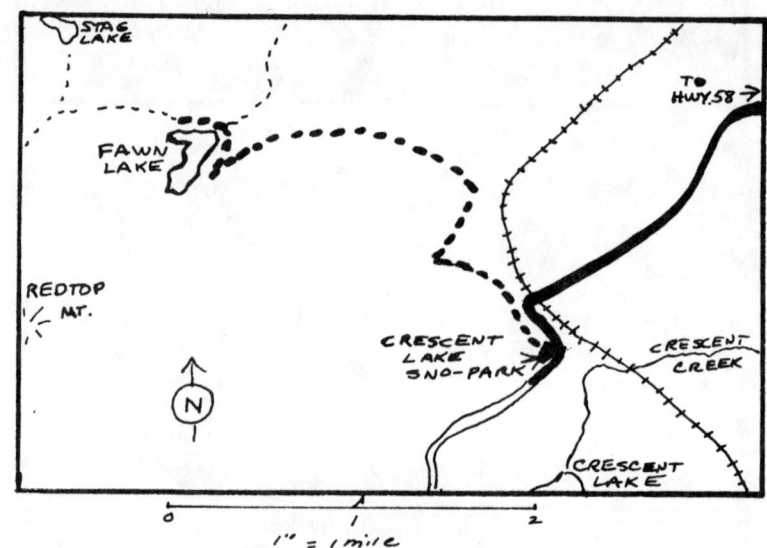

92 FAWN LAKE

from ODELL LAKE

STARTING POINT: Highway #58 to Odell Lake Resort at the east end of Odell Lake. Parking is near the lodge.

DISTANCE: 4 miles one way
ELEVATION: Odell Lake - 4,787'
            Fawn Lake - 5,600'
TERRAIN: Uphill, moderate to more difficult
MAPS: USDA Forest Service: Deschutes National Forest, Diamond Peak Wilderness
            USGS: Odell Lake, Oregon 7.5' 1963
                  Waldo Lake, Oregon 15' 1956

This is a marked ski trail starting near Odell Lake Resort. Ski a short distance to the Southern Pacific Railroad tracks.

The ski trail starts across the tracks. From here it goes uphill and through the woods all the way to Fawn Lake.

To make a loop tour, park a car at the Crescent Lake Townsite Sno-Park and leave one at Odell Lake. Ski whichever way you prefer. Loop tour is about eight miles.

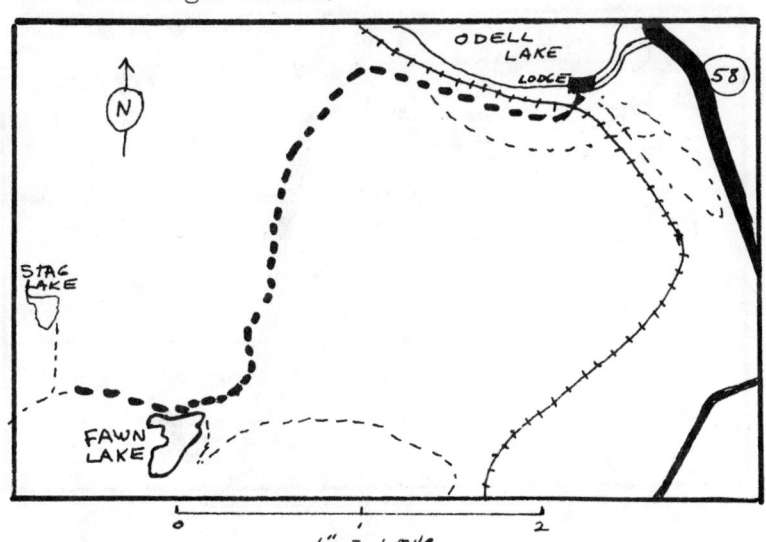

93 ODELL MEADOWS

STARTING POINT: Odell Lake Resort at the east end of Odell Lake from highway #58.

DISTANCE: Three miles of trails

ELEVATION: Odell Lake - 4,787'

TERRAIN: Easy, with "ups and downs" in the woods

MAPS: USDA Forest Service: Deschutes National Forest
USGS: Odell Lake, Oregon 7.5' 1963

This is a good beginner area. There are marked trails through the woods. Some trails make a loop. Most of the area is very gentle and quite level.

The trails go almost to the Crescent Lake landing strip, which is a wide open flat.

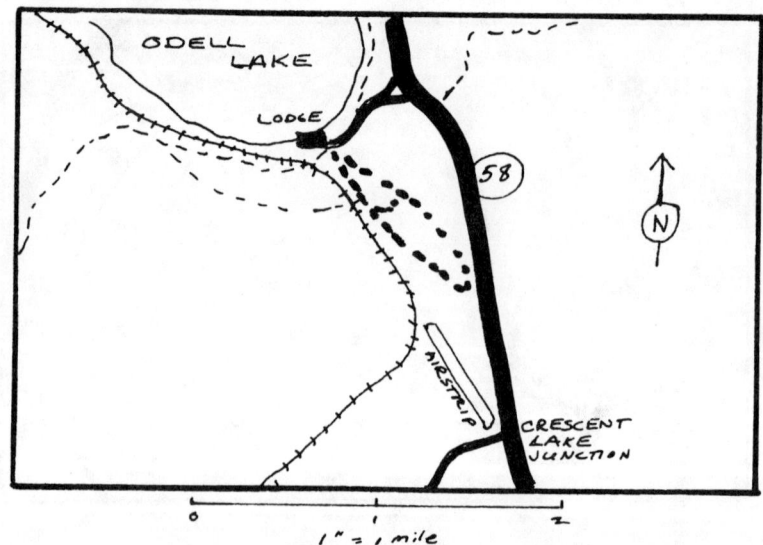

94 ODELL BUTTE

STARTING POINT: Drive south from Bend on highway #97 to Crescent. In the middle of town turn west on road #61. Follow this road for about 7 or 8 miles to the sign pointing to Odell Butte. Park off the side of the road.

DISTANCE: About 7 miles one way

ELEVATION: Road #61 - about 4,500'
Odell Butte - 7,032'

TERRAIN: Uphill on a road
MAPS: USDA Forest Service: Deschutes National Forest
USGS: Odell Butte, Oregon 7.5' 1967

Ski south from road #61 on the Odell Butte forest road. It is uphill all of the way and with good snow would be a good run back down.
From the top there is an excellent view of the area toward Diamond Peak, Crescent Lake and Odell Lake. Also on top, there is a forest service fire lookout and several electronic installations.

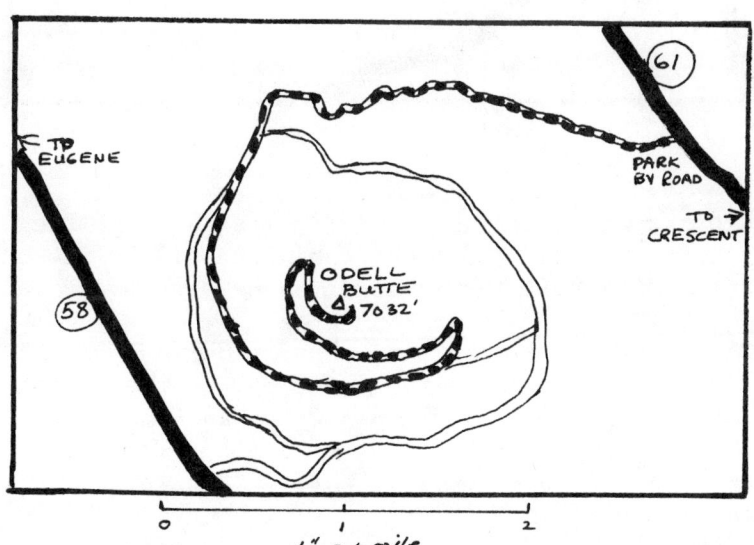

177

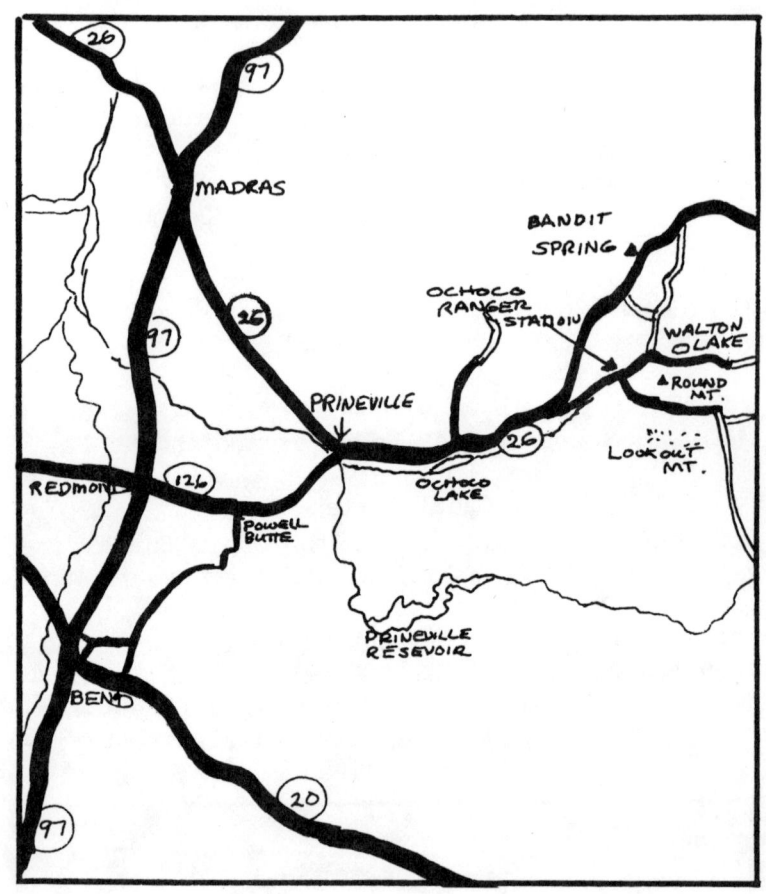

Cross country skiing activity is just getting started in the Ochoco National Forest. It is an area which will be developed as need arises.

The marked trails around Bandit Spring are the first. These are being developed by the Forest Service and the Nordic Ski Club in Prineville. Other skiing at this time in the Ochocos is mainly on forest roads or through the woods with map and compass.

Skiing in the Ochocos

SECTION 10
OCHOCOS

No.		Page
95.	Bandit Spring	180
96.	Southside - Marks Creek	181
97.	Crystal Springs	182
98.	Walton Lake.	184
99.	Road 200 - Blue Ridge Mine and Round Mountain	186
100.	Lookout Mountain	188

95 BANDIT SPRING

STARTING POINT: East from Prineville on highway #26. Bandit Spring is a roadside rest stop about one mile west of the Ochoco Divide. Limited parking is in the plowed turnout.

DISTANCE: Short loop - about 1 1/2 miles
Longer loop - about 5 1/2 miles

ELEVATION: Bandit Spring - about 4,550'
High point of trail - abt. 5,200'

TERRAIN: Short loop - easy, gentle sloping
Longer loop - more difficult

MAPS: USDA Forest Service: Ochoco National Forest
USGS: Lookout Mt., Oregon 15' 1951

SHORT LOOP (A Loop):
The short loop can be skied in either direction without too much difficulty. The terrain is very easy to moderate, depending upon snow conditions. It is open woods of Ponderosa Pine. This trail starts out up the forest road from the parking area. The first part of the loop is to the right shortly past the gate. The other part of this loop is on up the same road a short distance further and to the right.

LONGER LOOP (B Loop):
The longer loop is best skied counter-clockwise. Start out by skiing up either part of the short loop. Then continue on up the fairly steep hillside on the marked route to road #27. The trail follows road #27 for about 1/2 mile to the high point of this trail. Watch for the trail to turn downhill through the woods. This trail then comes out on another forest road which follows downhill, almost to highway #26. Just before the main highway, the trail turns left through the trees to paralled the highway back to Bandit Spring.

ROAD #27:
About one-half mile past Bandit Spring is road #27 which goes northeast from the highway. There is no parking here, but it can be reached on skis from Bandit Spring by skiing through the woods. This road leads up the ridge to a view point which is 6,181'. It is about five miles up to the viewpoint.

96 SOUTH SIDE

SOUTHSIDE:
Across highway #26 from Bandit Spring is an open flat along Marks Creek. You can ski on the flat or back on to the several open hillsides accessible from here.

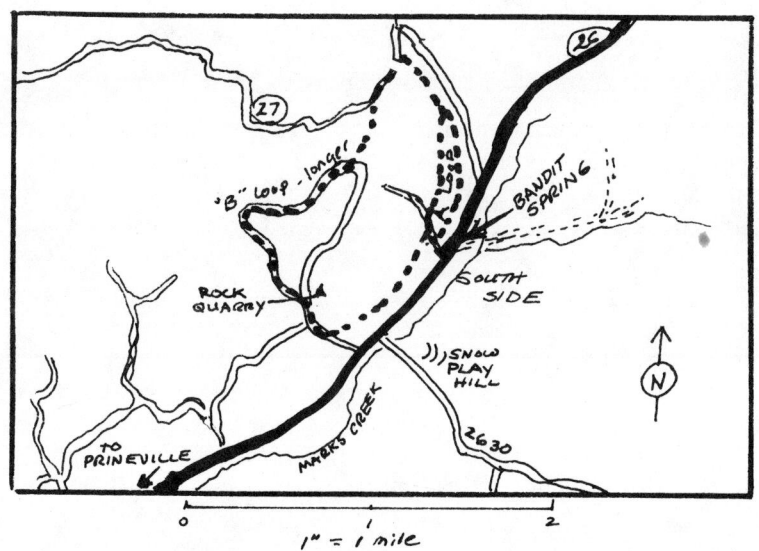

97 CRYSTAL SPRINGS

STARTING POINT: Park either at Bandit Spring roadside rest stop, or about 1/2 mile west of there, where road #2630 goes southeast. (There is also a sledding hill here.)

DISTANCE: As far as you wish on forest roads

ELEVATION: Bandit Spring - about 4,550'
Crystal Springs - about 4,650'
Jct. of roads #2630 & #2210 - 5,078'

TERRAIN: Gentle forest roads

MAPS: USDA Forest Service: Ochoco National Forest
USGS: Lookout Mt., Oregon 15' 1951

There are no marked ski trails here as yet, however there are many miles of forest roads which make good ski trails. Use your map and start out on road #2630, then ski as far as you want.

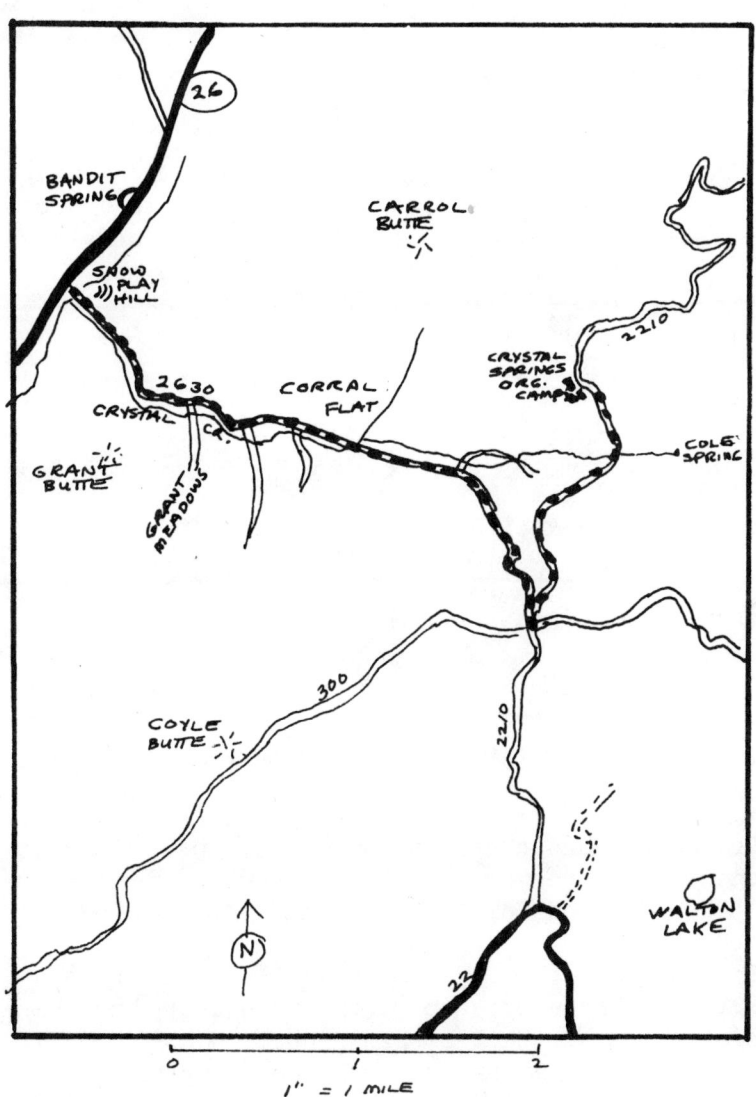

98 WALTON LAKE

STARTING POINT: East from Prineville on highway #26. Then right on road #22 to Ochoco Ranger Station. Continue on road #22 to junction of #2210. If the road is plowed there is usually parking at this junction.

DISTANCE: From junction of #22 & #2210 to Walton Lake - about 2 1/2 miles
Around Walton Lake - about 1 mile

ELEVATION: Walton Lake - about 5,200'
Jct. of #22 & #2210 - about 4,880'

TERRAIN: Uphill on the road

MAPS: USDA Forest Service: Ochoco National Forest
USGS: Lookout Mountain, Ore. 15' 1951

Access to this area is dependent upon whether the road is plowed or not. Check with the Ochoco Ranger Station for this information. (447-3845)

The easiest way to Walton Lake is to ski up road #22. After about two miles, turn left down the road into Walton Lake Campground. Road #2220 goes around the lake through the campground. Be careful about skiing on the lake. Ice at this elevation may not be very solid.

Another short little ski trip from this same parking spot is to ski up road #050. It starts out up a drainage, and then on to a ridge. It is a forest road.

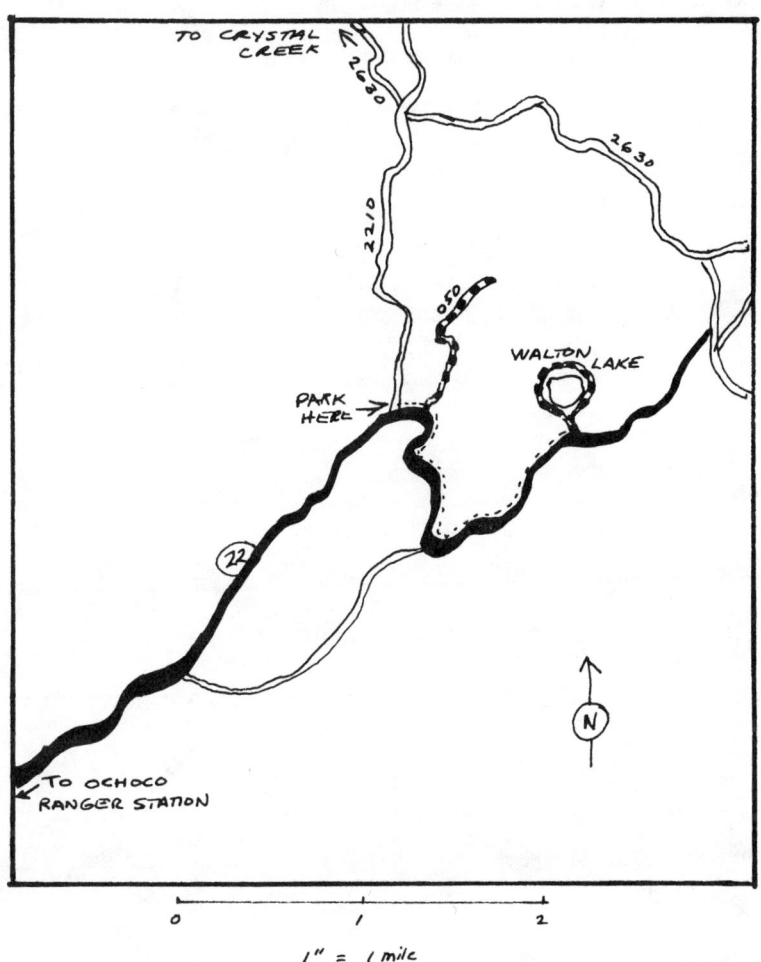

99 ROAD 200

BLUE RIDGE MINE
ROUND MOUNTAIN

STARTING POINT: East from Prineville on highway #26. Right on road #22 to Ochoco Ranger Station. Just past the ranger station, go right on road #42. About 12 miles or so farther, there is parking by an old house (Blue Ridge Mine) if the road is plowed. This is over the summit, and past Amity Mine.

DISTANCE: As far as you like on forest roads

ELEVATION: At parking, roads #42 & #200 - 4,732'

TERRAIN: Gentle forest roads

MAPS: USDA Forest Service: Ochoco National Forest
USGS: Lookout Mountain, Ore. 15' 1951

Check with the Ochoco Ranger Station to see if the road #42 is plowed. (447-3845)

From parking by the old house at the old Blue Ridge Mine, road #200 starts uphill behind the house. There are no marked ski trails, but there are a number of good forest roads to explore. Road #210 makes a loop of about 4 miles back to road #42. Walk 1/2 mile back to your car.

Other roads continue on up in the vicinity of Round Mountain.

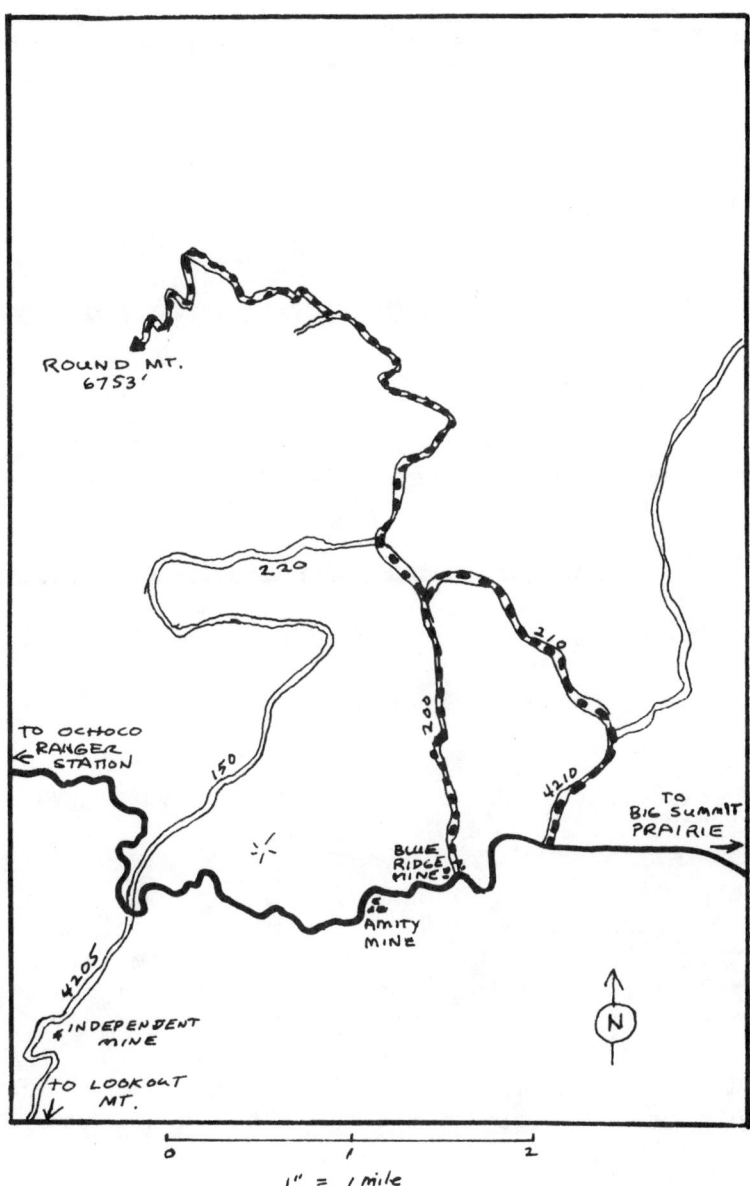

100 LOOKOUT MOUNTAIN

STARTING POINT: East from Prineville on highway #26. Right on road #22 to Ochoco Ranger Station. Just past the ranger station to right on road #42. If the road is plowed, there will probably be parking at road #4205 (Independent Mine Rd).

DISTANCE: About 3 1/2 miles one way

ELEVATION: Jct. of #42 & #4205 - about 5,440'
Lookout Mountain - 6,926'

TERRAIN: Steep uphill (old road)
This is a trail for advanced skiers.

MAPS: USDA Forest Service: Ochoco National Forest
USGS: Lookout Mountain, Ore. 15' 1951

Check with the Ochoco Ranger Station (447-3845) to find out if road #42 is plowed.

Lookout Mountain is a special management area, which means it is used by backpackers, hikers, etc. in the summer, with no motorized vehicles. In winter snowmobiles are allowed in the area, so watch for them on the road.

There is no marked ski trail. Ski up road #4205 which goes steeply to the top of Lookout Mountain. Along the way, you will pass the old Independent Mine. On top of the mountain is an open ridge.

Since the downhill run back is steep, this is a trail for advanced skiers.

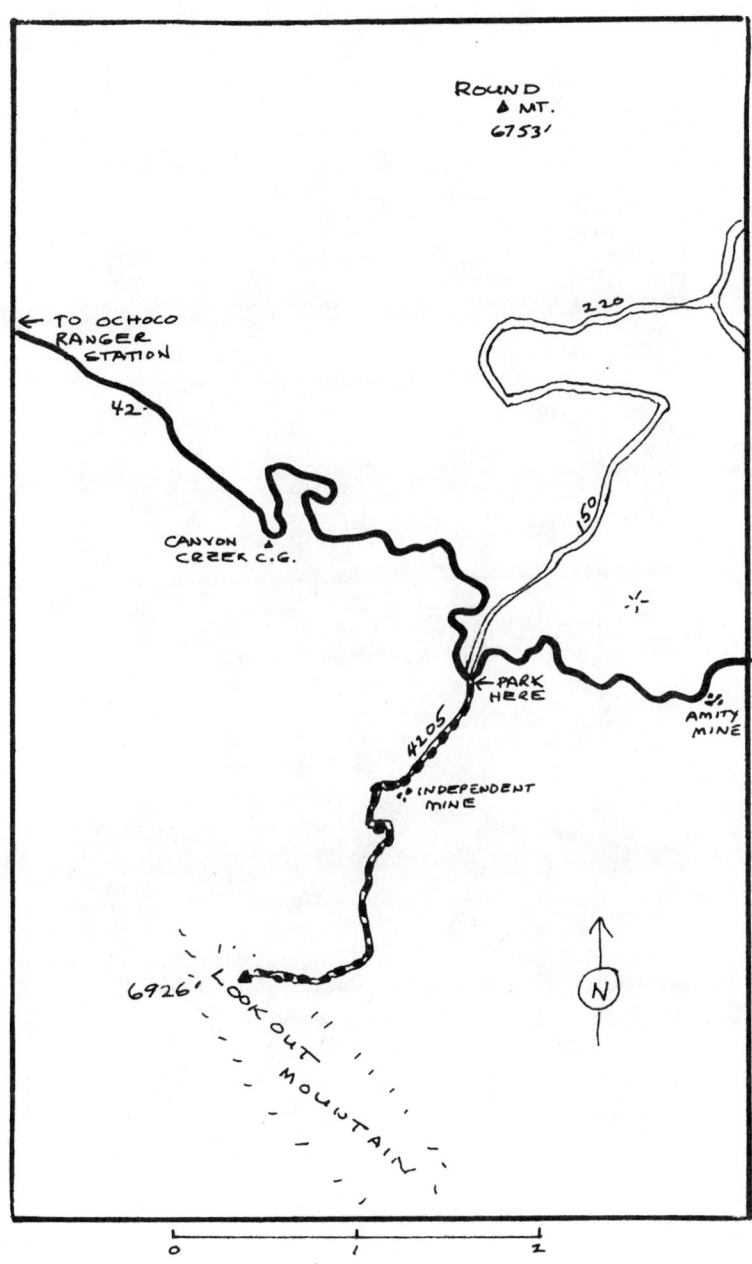

Wind blown tree on a mountain top

RESORTS AND SKI AREAS WITH
CROSS COUNTRY SKIING TRAILS:

  Mt. Bachelor Ski Area

  Sunriver Resort

  Hoodoo Ski Bowl

  Willamette Pass Ski Area

  Shelter Cove Resort

  Odell Lake Lodge

  Paulina Lake Lodge

  Elk Lake Resort

Broken Top Cirque

To order additional copies write to:

    Meissner Books
    P.O. Box 5296
    Bend, Oregon 97708

Enclose payment of $ 7.95
Postage & handling <u>1.00</u>

Total $ 8.95